Christmas
1979

Kristyn,
Hope this book helps
answer your inquisitiveness.
Love,
Mom & Dad

Answers
for Young
Latter-day
Saints

Answers
for Young
Latter-day
Saints

Published by
Deseret Book Company
Salt Lake City, Utah
1977

© 1977 by Deseret Book Co.
All Rights Reserved
ISBN 0-87747-645-4

Library of Congress Cataloging in Publication Data

Main entry under title:
Answers for young Latter-day Saints.

    Includes index.
    SUMMARY: A collection of answers to doctrinal and social
questions raised by young adult members of the Church of Jesus
Christ of Latter-day Saints.
    1. Youth—Religious life—Addresses, essays, lectures.
2. Church of Jesus Christ of Latter-day Saints—Doctrinal and
controversial works—Juvenile literature—Addresses, essays,
lectures.   [1. Conduct of life.   2. Church of Jesus
Christ of Latter-day Saints—Doctrinal and controversial works]
I. New Era (Salt Lake City)   II. Church of Jesus
Christ of Latter-day Saints.
BX8643.Y6A57   248'.83   77-3284
ISBN 0-87747-645-4

Contents

1   How can I know if I have a testimony?
G. Homer Durham

3   Does God hear everyone's prayers?
Roger Merrill

6   How can the Savior be a personal counselor to me?
Dean Jarman

8   Can Satan or his hosts read our thoughts? And do they still have a knowledge of our pre-earth life, which knowledge could and would aid them in tempting us?
Elder ElRay L. Christiansen

11   In my particular college environment where I am exposed to strong attitudes of atheism, how can I protect my religious beliefs and still get good grades?
Lowell G. Tensmeyer

12   Why can't we have a youth movement in the Church in which we campaign for causes that the Church espouses or permits us to espouse?
Bishop Victor L. Brown

14   Is there any similarity between existentialism and the gospel?
Mae Blanch

15   Which is more compatible with the Church, liberalism or conservatism?
G. Homer Durham

16   My ecology class in school is very critical of people who are selfish enough to bring more than two children into the world when it is becoming overpopulated and so highly polluted. How can I answer this?
Howard M. Bahr

22   I don't feel "in" with religion. What difference does it make if I enjoy X-rated movies and novels of contemporary morality standards?
Arthur R. Bassett

23   Can people who build so many fences around certain experiences, such as no smoking, no drinking, and no immorality, ever be real artists? Mustn't the artist almost by definition live either totally without fences or with only makeshift, empirical fences-of-the-moment?
Carol Lynn Pearson

25   How does one know when he is becoming a fanatic on a principle and letting things get out of balance?
Rodney Turner

26   Are certain forms of creative art discouraged in the Church, such as modern visual art and modern dance?
Edward D. Maryon

27   What are the reasons for and the process of excommunication?
Elder Robert L. Simpson

30   What kind of emphasis should we as Latter-day Saints place on intellectual activities and pursuits?
Karen Lynn

33   Is it necessary for us to have four years of college?
William R. Siddoway

34   Is religious education more important than academic education?
J. Elliott Cameron

35   Is it justifiable to borrow money for educational purposes?
Joe J. Christensen

36   Because we believe in the principle of service, shouldn't a Latter-day Saint orient his vocation more to the field of public service?
Elder Marion D. Hanks

37   When does a missionary receive the keys for his ministry— when he is ordained an elder, when he is set apart for his mission, or when he receives his endowment?
J. Murray Rawson

38   How is the missionary's place of assignment determined?
President Spencer W. Kimball

39   When should a young man *not* go on a mission?
Elder Gordon B. Hinckley

40   Is it advisable to wait for a missionary?
Elder Loren C. Dunn

41   Should girls go on missions?
Arthur S. Anderson

43   Is it right to stress marriage right after a mission?
Ernest L. Eberhard, Jr.

44   How does the principle of presidency work in Aaronic
Priesthood quorums?
Robert L. Backman

47   How can I get my parents to understand that I feel
different than they do about some things?
Ernest L. Eberhard, Jr.

49   To whom should we go for help with our problems,
particularly those dealing with use of drugs?
Victor L. Brown, Jr.

51   How should we deal with friends who are taking drugs?
How can we help them?
Victor L. Brown, Jr.

52   Why can't I date when I am fifteen? I have nonmember
friends who are permitted to date at this same age.
Elder Vaughn J. Featherstone

55   Should a young girl date boys who are not members of the
Church if she lives in a small branch or ward where there
are few or no Latter-day Saint boys?
Lenore Romney

55   Should we pray with our dates before going out, while we
are out on a date, or when we come home?
Ardeth G. Kapp

58   What standards should I have in dating? Am I expected to
show affection for a girl on our first date, such as putting
my arm around her? What is the proper thing to do?
Joe J. Christensen

59   Are Latter-day Saint girls exempt from standards of
modesty in dress while they are performing in marching or
cheerleading groups?
Marilyn Arnold

60   Is it all right for a Latter-day Saint girl to hitchhike? When would it not be acceptable? I hitchhiked recently to my university during a bus strike.
Marilyn Arnold

62   What is the purpose of courtship, and what is the ideal length of time a couple should go together before they get married?
William Rolfe Kerr

64   How can I know when I have found the right person to marry?
Darwin L. Thomas

67   What are the requirements for a person to receive a temple recommend for marriage?
Malcolm S. Jeppsen

70   What is a temple endowment? When is it recommended that a Church member receive the endowment? Can a twenty-one-year-old girl who plans to be married in the temple in the near future receive her endowment prior to the marriage date?
John K. Edmunds

75   What can you tell me about the temple marriage ceremony?
Robert L. Backman

77   My parents are not active in the Church and will be unable to attend my temple wedding. Since I did not serve a mission and do not have other relatives who are members of the Church, will there be someone in the temple to help me so I will know what to do, where to go, etc.?
Mary Clarke

79   Will I be allowed to wear my wedding dress to my temple marriage or sealing? If so, are there special requirements that I need to know about before my marriage so I can design my dress accordingly?
Jasmine R. Edmunds

81   What happens when a couple get a temple divorce? What happens to the children in the next life?
Elder James A. Cullimore

82   Do early marriages tend to end in failure?
Darwin L. Thomas

86   Should a girl worry about not getting married?
     Alberta H. Christensen

87   How do women share the priesthood? How does it apply
     to an unmarried woman?
     Hortense H. Child

89   What kinds of activities are acceptable on the Sabbath?
     Russell C. Harris

91   Should I pay tithing on money my parents give me if they
     have already paid tithing on that money?
     Bishop Victor L. Brown

92   Why is fasting so important and how can we make it
     work?
     Stephen R. Covey

95   Is it against Church standards to drink cola beverages or
     any other beverage containing caffeine?
     Bishop H. Burke Peterson

97   My nonmember friends seem to know a lot about the
     Church's financial system and business interests. They say
     we own controlling interests in many national companies,
     some of which manufacture products that are against our
     standards, such as liquor and tobacco. What should I tell
     them?
     President N. Eldon Tanner

98   Should college students and other single persons get
     involved in food storage programs?
     Winnifred Jardine

99   Should a nonmember take the sacrament when attending
     church with a member?
     Elder Loren C. Dunn

100 Why have we been told not to use playing cards?
     Elder William H. Bennett

102 Is there any reason or Church doctrine that would suggest
     that I should not have my ears pierced?
     Marianne C. Sharp

103 What do you think about the use of hypnotism?
     Homer Ellsworth

105   Are there ever any circumstances that justify not accepting a Church position?
Bishop Victor L. Brown

106   What can be done to make gospel lessons more interesting?
Charles R. Hobbs

108   How can I profit more from stake conference? Lately I've begun to feel that going to conference is a waste of my time.
Richard H. Morley

This book is a compilation of questions asked by young members of The Church of Jesus Christ of Latter-day Saints and answered in the *New Era* by Church leaders and members. These questions deal with the concerns of today's youth regarding their role in the Church, in the family, and in society.

Although the questions originally appeared in a Church-sponsored magazine, the answers are intended for perspective and insight and not as pronouncements of Church doctrine.

Every conscious human being has a testimony of many things—that fire is hot, ice is cold, people are kind and unkind. A testimony is a declaration or affirmation to establish some fact.

A testimony of the truth of the gospel of Jesus Christ comes, fundamentally, in the same way that one learns about natural phenomena and human behavior, namely, by desire, effort, experience, and learning, including study, reflection, practice, and testing. In learning anything, it is always beneficial to make effort intelligently and with purpose. Jesus taught: "If any man will do his will, he shall know of the doctrine. . . ." (John 7:17.) James wrote: "If any of you lack wisdom, let him ask of God, that giveth to all men liberally. . . ." (James 1:5.)

A testimony of the truth of Christ's gospel as restored by the Prophet Joseph Smith—that God lives, hears, and answers prayers, that Jesus Christ is the Savior of the world, that he guides and directs the Church through authorized priesthood channels, and that divine guidance is available to everyone who seeks it—can come in many ways and through a variety of experiences. Generally, the ability, willingness, and confidence one has in making such a solemn declaration comes from (1) desire, (2) study, (3) work, and (4) prayer. Study opens the door to knowledge. Before we can do his will, we must first come to know it. Work, or the application of the knowledge gained, using it in practice, is the laboratory in which knowledge can be tested. Prayer, accompanying both study and work, sustains intelligent, purposeful efforts and brings the confirmation of the Holy Spirit.

How do you know if you have such a testimony?

The best way to find out is to express your honest, innermost feelings. Don't undertake to amplify your doubts, but express those things of which you have hope. Expression is one form of doing. Express yourself to a parent, another loved one, a friend, a trusted counselor or teacher such as the bishop. Your first effort at stating your solemn declaration and affirmation will probably impress you with the fact that inside, after all, you really know for yourself more than you realized beforehand. Do not overlook the promises in the Book of Mormon and the Doctrine and Covenants:

"And when ye shall receive these things, I would exhort you that ye would ask God, the Eternal Father, in the name of

Christ, if these things are not true; and if ye shall ask with a sincere heart, with real intent, having faith in Christ, he will manifest the truth of it unto you, by the power of the Holy Ghost.

"And by the power of the Holy Ghost ye may know the truth of all things.

"And whatsoever thing is good is just and true; wherefore, nothing that is good denieth the Christ, but acknowledgeth that he is." (Moroni 10:4-6.)

"Behold, you have not understood; you have supposed that I would give it unto you, when you took no thought save it was to ask me.

"But, behold, I say unto you, that you must study it out in your mind; then you must ask me if it be right, and if it is right I will cause that your bosom shall burn within you; therefore, you shall feel that it is right.

"But if it be not right you shall have no such feelings, but you shall have a stupor of thought that shall cause you to forget the thing which is wrong; therefore, you cannot write that which is sacred save it be given you from me." (D&C 9:7-9.)

If you have faithfully studied, worked, and prayed, you will *know,* just as you know when you feel well, or unwell. As Moroni wrote, ". . . by the power of the Holy Ghost ye may know the truth of all things."

President Brigham Young said: "Now, my friends . . . how do you know anything? Can you be deceived by the eye? You can. . . . Can you be deceived in hearing? Yes; you may hear sounds but not understand their import or whence they come. Can you be deceived by the touch of the fingers? You can. The nervous system will not detect everything. What will? The revelations of the Lord Jesus Christ, the spirit of truth will detect everything, and enable all who possess it to understand truth from error, light from darkness, the things of God from the things not of God. It is the only thing that will enable us to understand the Gospel of the Son of God, the will of God, and how we can be saved. Follow it, and it will lead to God, the fountain of light, where the gate will be open, and the mind will be enlightened so that we shall see, know and understand things as they are." (*Discourses of Brigham Young,* 1946 ed., p. 34.)

Finally, you should not expect a thunderbolt or some extraordinary manifestation. Rather, a testimony, in most cases, grows. It unfolds gradually, as it is desired, cultivated, and fed.

But you will know. And it will be up to you to keep it sturdy and strong. If you neglect it or discard your desire and exchange it for other values, or if you merely drift, your testimony will diminish. If you forsake it and pursue other values, one day you will not know the truth of the gospel. You will not manifest and declare your knowledge of it, because you yourself will have moved away and rejected it. Those who, like Saul of Tarsus on the road to Damascus, receive direct, divine intervention are few in number. Nevertheless, help from those who have firm convictions is always available. But ultimately each person has to determine and decide for himself. Then without hesitation one may clearly affirm his knowledge. As study, activity, and prayer continue, one discovers the meaning of Doctrine and Covenants 50:24: "That which is of God is light; *and he that receiveth light, and continueth in God,* receiveth more light; and that light groweth brighter and brighter until the perfect day." (Italics added.) —*G. Homer Durham*

Does God hear everyone's prayers?

There are at least two different approaches people might take in response to this question. One approach is exemplified by a young man we will call Eric. People tell Eric that he is very smart, and he prides himself on his ability to think through ideas and explain them to others.

Recently Eric has been studying about the different nations of the earth. One afternoon as he was watching a film in school about the eastern countries, he was deeply impressed with the number of people on the earth and how varied their lives are. He asked himself, Does God really hear everyone's prayers? After pondering for a while he could not conceive how one being could really listen to all those prayers at one time. "It is just impossible. He must have angels assigned to listen for him," he reasoned. This answer was logical but somehow it made him feel a little farther away from his Father in heaven.

Richard is a good example of another approach. Born in the Church, he was not active until he was well into his teens. At that time a series of challenging events provided him with the opposition necessary to turn him toward the gospel. After a few weeks of reading and praying, Richard had developed a testimony of Christ and the truth of the Book of Mormon. People remembered him because of his testimony and his commitment to it.

One evening Eric and Richard were talking about the Church. Eric said, "You know, one thing that bothers me about the Church is that it demands so much blind obedience."

"What do you mean?" asked Richard.

"Well, for example, the other day in class we were talking about prayer, and I mentioned how many people there are in the world and said that God can't possibly hear all those prayers. He must have others do it for him. Brother Edwards said I was wrong, and I asked how he knew. He quoted a bunch of scriptures. Boy, what a cop-out—just blind faith."

"That's really interesting, but I disagree on the blind faith idea," replied Richard. "I thought about that same question not long ago. The first thing I asked myself was, What has the Lord already said about it? I read some passages in the Doctrine and Covenants (see D&C 88:62-63) and also found a great statement by President John Taylor:

" 'We are told in relation to these matters that the hairs of our heads are numbered; that even a sparrow cannot fall to the ground without our heavenly Father's notice; and predicated upon some of these principles are some things taught by Jesus, where he tells men to ask and they shall receive. What! the millions that live upon the earth? Yes, the millions of people, no matter how many there are. Can he hear and answer all? Can he attend to all these things? Yes.' (*Journal of Discourses* 26:31.)

"Since I already have a testimony of the scriptures and the living prophets, the next thing I wanted to know was what do I have to do in order to understand more about *how* God hears and answers prayers. I've been praying about it, and last fast Sunday afternoon I was reading Doctrine and Covenants 88 about the Light of Christ and how it is in and through all things. Of course, I know our Father in heaven is a distinct personage, but this taught that his power, spirit, glory, and influence emanate throughout the universe and create a channel through which light and life are given to all that live. As I've been thinking about this, I think I'm starting to realize how our Father can be in personal contact with all his children. I've concluded that God hears all who pray, but for us to receive his answers, we must live the commandments and seek him. I don't feel that that is blind faith."

Richard's conclusion meets a great test because it fits with what President Harold B. Lee said in a talk on revelation. He said that we are much like a radio receiver: if our tithing tube is broken, or our keep-morally-clean tube is not operating correctly, we will never receive the messages the Lord sends. Even worse, we could be on the wrong station, thinking we are receiving messages from the Lord when all the time they are coming from the wrong source.

There is an old Chinese proverb that says, in effect, it is not knowing all the answers that indicates a man's wisdom, but in knowing how to ask the right questions. What are the right questions and how does that relate to prayer? Prayer is communication between God and man. When we approach the Lord in prayer to seek knowledge and wisdom, our questions should be *faithful* questions.

Faithful questions seek to understand rather than judge. When Joseph Smith was searching, he read in James 1:5, "If any of you lack wisdom, let him ask of God, that giveth to all men liberally, and upbraideth not; and it shall be given him." Joseph also read (which we sometimes forget), "But let him ask in faith, nothing wavering." The scripture goes on to say of one who wavers and doubts, " . . . let not that man think that he shall receive any thing of the Lord."

Richard knew how to ask questions; Eric did not. The difference? "But let him ask in faith, nothing wavering."

Eric asked a prejudgmental challenging question that was not based on trust and faith in the things he had already received. "Let not that man think that he shall receive any thing of the Lord."

Richard did not seek to judge, but to understand. It is with faith and trust that we can learn to follow President Lee's counsel to put periods after what the Lord has said, not question marks. Faith in seeking brings knowledge, wisdom, and light.

I affirm that God does hear all our prayers; he loves us and seeks to communicate. We need to learn to ask the right questions and, in the things of God especially, seek to understand, not to judge.—*Roger Merrill*

*How can the Savior
be a personal counselor to me?*

*T*his question suggests a belief in a wonderful relationship with the Savior in which one senses his nearness, his love, and his guidance. In this setting men can counsel with the Lord and receive direction from his influence.

A question that is often asked is, How can this happen—especially to me? The scriptures teach us about the counseling relationship one can have with the Savior. There is an influence or Spirit that comes from Christ to every individual. It is often called the Light of Christ, the Spirit of Christ, or sometimes even the word of the Lord. (D&C 84:44-45.) This influence is one of guidance and enlightenment.

The Lord instructed Joseph Smith that "the Spirit giveth light to every man that cometh into the world; and the Spirit enlighteneth every man through the world, that hearkeneth to the voice of the Spirit." (D&C 84:46.) Some refer to the Light of Christ as one's true conscience. That is, there is something within each person that is of Christ; it is a true light or true conscience. As we hearken to the true voice or feeling within us, the promise of the Lord is that a spiritual enlightenment will occur, or, in other words, an increase of light. Our understanding of what is right will increase, and we will come more to enjoy the mind of Christ.

Often when an individual tries to solve a problem, he relies heavily on his ability to think, to consider alternatives, and to weigh the consequences of possible choices. This is a valuable process but is incomplete by itself. We need also to search and listen to the truest feelings within ourselves, which feelings are the Light of Christ. There can be many voices that speak to us, but there is one true light within that is of Christ. Let me illustrate this idea with three examples.

A returned missionary came one day for some advice on whether he should join a particular group on campus. When asked what he thought about it, he suggested several ideas that seemed to point to one course of action. When asked what he really felt *inside* about it, there was at first a look of puzzlement and then a smile as he recognized that the feeling was different from what most of his reasons suggested.

One day a boy stopped by my office and for several moments talked very negatively and critically about the Church, suggesting several reasons why the Church just couldn't be the Lord's. When asked to search deeply within himself, to examine his conscience concerning the matter as to whether or not the Church was the Lord's, he replied after some reflective thought, "I feel it is true."

Another individual was advocating a course of immorality, suggesting that a boy and girl are free to choose the nature of their affectional relationship based on the circumstances of each situation, without fear of law or punishment, neither of which he felt existed. He was confronted with God's standard of morality and the truth that there is something within each person that comes from the Lord to assist him in distinguishing between good and evil. When he was challenged to look within himself to see which of the two conflicting approaches to morality was really right, he replied, after some pause, "That which I feel is different from that which I have been saying."

Yes, truly did Mormon write that "the Spirit of Christ is given to every man, that he may know good from evil. . . ." He further said that the true way to judge is to be able to discern one's feelings, "for every thing which inviteth to do good . . . is sent forth by the power and gift of Christ. . . ." (Moroni 7:16.)

The reflective thought within us must be sincere and have real intent. Many times an individual will lay aside the influence of the Lord in favor of what seems appealing or rational at the moment. Such an individual may fluctuate back and forth in his feelings. If the negative feelings are a true source of inspiration, they will continue to be felt if one really wants to know what he should do.

On one occasion a girl was trying to decide whether or not to marry a certain individual and was confused because at times she felt doubt and uncertainty and at other times was certain she wanted to marry him. When they were together it seemed right, but when she was alone or away from him, there was much doubt and uncertainty. We talked about many things: the kind of person she wanted to marry, the element of trust in marriage, possible reasons for her doubt, and why at times it seemed all right. Toward the end of the conversation she was asked to consider what she really felt was the right thing to do. After a few moments she observed that she had really known all along that it wasn't right but had just put aside those feelings. We must follow the counsel of Mormon and "search diligently in the light of Christ that ye may know good from evil. . . ." He then promised, ". . . if ye will lay hold upon every good thing, and condemn it not, ye certainly will be a child of Christ." (Moroni 7:19.)

In developing a counseling relationship with Christ, follow these three simple processes: (1) recognize and believe that there is a feeling within you that comes from Christ; (2) consider the alternatives; and (3) listen to your honest feelings. If you are in doubt, then it is usually wise not to proceed. When you follow your true conscience, there will be an attendant joy and peace. The old adage of "follow your conscience" is true and applicable in learning to discern and follow the counsel of the Savior.——
Dean Jarman

*Can Satan or his hosts
read our thoughts?
And do they still have
a knowledge of our pre-earth life,
which knowledge could
and would aid them
in tempting us?*

The account of Satan, or Lucifer, is a frightening example of rebellion against God and apostasy from that which is right.

All of us, including Lucifer, are sons and daughters of God. Before we were born into mortality, we lived in the premortal state as spirit children of our heavenly parents. There we were taught the plan of salvation.

We learn from the scriptures that Lucifer, a brilliant, influential character who had considerable authority in the premortal world, rebelled against the Father's plan whereby man was to come to earth and have his free agency. He declared: "Behold, here am I, send me, I will be thy son, and I will redeem all mankind, that one soul shall not be lost, and surely I will do it; wherefore give me thine honor."

Jesus Christ, however, accepted the Father's plan, saying, "Father, thy will be done, and the glory be thine forever." (Moses 4:1-2.) As we know, Jesus Christ was selected to become the Savior and Redeemer of mankind, and we were given our free agency in mortality.

Lucifer's proposal, based on forcible compliance to law, was rejected; and one-third of the heavenly host also rebelled and vowed allegiance to him. They and he were cast out and denied forever the blessing of mortal bodies. "And he became Satan, yea, even the devil, the father of all lies, to deceive and to blind men, and to lead them captive at his will, even as many as would not hearken unto my voice." (Moses 4:4.)

We must realize Satan, the devil, lives just as certainly as we live. Those who teach that there is no devil are simply unaware of the facts. Satan lives. The rebellious spirits who followed him live. Even though they are denied the blessing of possessing mortal bodies, they possess great power to deceive and to destroy our free agency and take away peace. Satan has declared war against the saints and will destroy our standards and even our souls, if he can. (D&C 76:29.)

True Christians know that invisible forces are waging war against God and his people who are striving to do his will. Being cast out of heaven, Satan and his hosts turned to the tactics of temptation, deception, and lies. He commenced by intruding into the household of Adam and causing Cain to become a murderer—to shed the blood of his own brother, Abel. He even tried to entice our Redeemer through tempting him, but Jesus resisted, and Satan failed.

Because of the Prophet Joseph Smith's role in bringing about a restoration of the gospel in this dispensation, he became Satan's target. Satan did all in his power to destroy Joseph just before the appearance of the Father and the Son in the Sacred Grove. Joseph wrote:

". . . I kneeled down and began to offer up the desire of my heart to God. I had scarcely done so, when immediately I was seized upon by some power which entirely overcame me . . . as to bind my tongue so that I could not speak." (Joseph Smith 2:15.)

God allows Lucifer and his agents to tempt us so that we may more deliberately choose between good and evil. The Lord could banish Satan and his angels from the earth and remove temptations from men, but "it must needs be that the devil should tempt the children of men, or they could not be agents unto themselves; for if they never should have bitter they could not know the sweet." (D&C 29:39.)

Satan knows all the tricks. He knows where we are susceptible to temptations and how to entice us to do evil. He and his messengers suggest evil, minimize the seriousness of sin, and make evil inviting.

"He will appear to us in the person of a friend or a relative in whom we have confidence. He has power to place thoughts in our minds and to whisper to us in unspoken impressions to entice us to satisfy our appetites or carnal desires and in various ways he plays upon our weaknesses and desires." (Joseph Fielding Smith, *Melchizedek Priesthood Course of Study,* 1972-73, p. 298.)

Surely, then, Satan and his followers have some knowledge of our thoughts and tendencies. He has knowledge that is superior to man's knowledge, but he lacks the wisdom to properly use his knowledge for good purposes. Some people are like that and often find themselves opposing even that which is right and true. Satan is a great deceiver, a liar. He appeared unto Korihor in the form of an angel and said unto him: "Go and reclaim this people [the faithful believers in God], for they have all gone astray after an unknown God. And he said unto me: There is no God; yea, and he taught me that which I should say. And I have taught his words; and I taught them because they were pleasing unto the carnal mind; and I taught them, even until I had much success, insomuch that I verily believed that they were true; and for this cause I withstood the truth, even until I have brought this great curse upon me." (Alma 30:53.)

Satan and his aides no doubt may know our inclinations, our carnal tastes and desires, but they cannot compel a righteous person to do evil if he seeks help from the Lord. Too many try to blame Satan when in reality the fault lies within themselves because they yield to his enticements.

He delights in introducing to the world innovations and practices that lead to unhappiness and misery, all the while making it appear that such evil practices are now acceptable. "It is he who inspires every evil teaching, every evil thought even in false religions, creeds, and organizations." (*Teachings of the Prophet Joseph Smith,* p. 297.)

In the words of that great prophet Alma, "For I say unto you that whatsoever is good cometh from God, and whatsoever is evil cometh from the devil.

"Therefore, if a man bringeth forth good works he hearkeneth unto the voice of the good shepherd, and he doth follow him; but whosoever bringeth forth evil works, the same becometh a child of the devil, for he hearkeneth unto his voice, and doth follow him." (Alma 5:40-41.) —— *Elder ElRay L. Christiansen*

In my particular college environment
where I am exposed
to strong attitudes of atheism,
how can I protect my religious beliefs
and still get good grades?

Protecting grades from a prejudiced instructor is usually not difficult if we study a subject with interest and energy and without fear that learning will ruin our testimony. As a great man once told his now famous son, Henry Eyring, "You don't have to believe anything that isn't true to believe the gospel." But some of the things we religiously believe may need some alterations.

One of the purposes of college is to make us aware of what people throughout the world believe and why they believe it. We should learn to weigh evidence and remember its source, to know what we believe and why we believe it. College life and activities can help us get to know ourselves and our potential. They can also speed our fulfillment of the Lord's command to "seek . . . diligently . . . out of the best books words of wisdom." (D&C 88:118.)

In state-supported schools, church and state are legally separated, and instructors are supposed to give grades without respect to religious belief. Sometimes, however, a professor will teach a secular course almost as an expression of his own religion or lack of religion. He may feel that a student hasn't really seen the point of the course unless he loses his faith in God and places it elsewhere.

It may help to realize that intellectually we are not required to believe every theory or explanation that is presented to us. It is always good practice to include in class discussions and test answers such phrases as "fossil remains provide evidence that . . . ," or "Bertrand Russell taught that. . . ," or "We can infer from the similarities in proteins in living animals that. . . ." True-or-false and multiple-choice questions can be answered from the point of view of the evidence presented in the course.

If such questions have a meaning for religious faith, a wise person will weigh all the evidence he has from all sources and patiently seek more before changing his life-style. Religious faith is larger than any college course or series of courses.

We must remember, however, that destructive personal behavior is much more dangerous to religious faith than are new ideas. Wherever we are, we must avoid the actions that make us irreligious. Rationalizing wrong behavior can lead a person to "harden his heart." Then he no longer wants to listen to the voice within that tells him that God is his father. "Live so that you are not ashamed to be in the company of good people, and I'm sure the gospel will seem pretty wonderful to you." (Edward Eyring again.) So, seek out good companions.

Remember that the gospel is the truth; there is nothing weak about it. In contrast, though, a person's understanding of the gospel may only be a tender plant that needs to be fed with information and faithful associations. Our souls must come to know who we are through meditation and prayer. Only then can faith grow beyond the Junior Sunday School and junior high school levels.——*Lowell G. Tensmeyer*

*Why can't we have
a youth movement in the Church
in which we campaign
for causes that the Church espouses
or permits us to espouse?*

The Church has causes for which the youth of the Church campaign—but even more than campaigning, Latter-day Saint youths do something about these causes. To suggest that young Latter-day Saints do not espouse a cause indicates a lack of understanding of the Church youth program, which enlists its youth in many causes—from missionary work to the pursuit of education. No one should be espousing the cause of Jesus Christ more than we who have taken his name upon ourselves. But it is essential to understand the difference between many of the campaigns of the people of the world and the campaigns of Latter-day Saint youth under the direction of Church leadership. The Lord's house is a house of order. All of the activities of the members of the Church, if carried out through Church organization, must of necessity be carried out in an orderly manner.

It is also important to recognize that the Church is a church of action, not just words. An example of how the youth of the Church can function in espousing good causes was demonstrated a few years ago in the Salt Lake Valley. A black congregation had great difficulty in completing their chapel. They approached the leaders of our church for assistance. It was felt that this was a wonderful opportunity for our Aaronic Priesthood-age young men and women to band together and raise funds for others in need. Literally thousands of young Mormon men and women engaged in projects from washing cars to babysitting to mowing lawns in order to raise thousands of dollars to assist their neighbors. At the conclusion of the drive, a wonderful banquet was held with representatives from the various bishop's youth committees and the black congregation. There was no marching, carrying of banners, or loud oratory; but rather, in an orderly, enthusiastic spirit, under the direction of their own organizations, these Latter-day Saint youths demonstrated how other young Mormons can go about espousing a good cause—this one appropriately designated as "Operation Good Samaritan."

Society today seems to center its attention largely on the group that makes the loudest noise, overlooking the quiet group that gets things done. I would hope that the youth of the Church will not be concerned with the recognition of the world but rather will carry out in a quiet, orderly, dignified, effective way the injunction of the Savior to be "anxiously engaged in a good cause and do many things of their own free will, and bring to pass much righteousness." (D&C 58:27.)

The bishop's youth committee and the stake young adult leaders are the two councils that span the youth of the Church (twelve through twenty-six). Turn to your representatives on these councils and voice to them your desire to be involved in some good causes. I don't know of a single representative who would not welcome your participation.——*Bishop Victor L. Brown*

Is there any similarity between existentialism and the gospel?

Existentialism, the philosophy that has dominated Western thought since World War II, shares at least one important tenet with the gospel, although they differ sharply on their views on the nature of man. There are almost as many versions of existentialism as there are existentialist philosophers, but the one principle that they all start with can be summed up in the statement that existence is prior to essence. That is, the existentialists believe that man has no essence, no inherent eternal nature that defines him, prior to his existence. Thus man has the sole responsibility for determining through thought and action what his essence will be; man, through the exercise of free will, defines himself.

Existentialists claim that life has no meaning except that which man gives it, and it is therefore essential that man enjoy complete freedom to create his life so that it is a reflection of the truth as he has discovered it. To find his own truth, then, is an obligation no man can escape, and he must accomplish this with no outside help. Since in existentialist thought truth is relative, each man must determine his own; he cannot borrow that of someone else or even receive help from someone else in finding his own.

Mormon philosophy differs sharply from the existentialist in its view on the nature of man. Man is an eternal being; his nature already exists when he is born into this world and has existed for eternity. The highest potential for man has been defined by God through his prophets: " . . . as God is, man may become." The purpose of his life is to provide him with the opportunity to grow toward this goal. Life has a meaning ordained by God.

But like the existentialists, Latter-day Saints also place great emphasis on the necessity of freedom. Man must be free to make the choices that will lead him toward godhood. The Latter-day Saint does not determine his essence through thought and action, but he does determine his ultimate fate by these same means, and the sole responsibility is his. However, help is available to him in making these crucial choices. He has the help of parents, teachers of the gospel, leaders in the Church, the scriptures, and, most important of all, the Holy Ghost.

The differences between existential and Mormon views on the nature of man and the purpose of life are irreconcilable. For both philosophies, freedom is essential, free will a reality, and choice an imperative; but for the Latter-day Saint, a loving Father in heaven also offers help and direction.——*Mae Blanch*

*Which is more compatible
with the Church,*
~~ibrals~~ *liberalism or conservatism?* ⟩Republican

The question as submitted uses no adjectives, such as *political, economic,* or *religious.* This response assumes the question has been asked with political connotation. The terms *liberalism* and *conservatism* are much-abused terms. They have almost lost precise and useful meaning. In daily repartee both are often resorted to as cloaks for self-proclaimed righteousness or are used as efforts to stylize or categorize another's contrary position or views.

The Church moves ahead and has a mission to fulfill despite all political currents. It is a conservative institution, seeking to "hold fast to that which is good." It also stands for liberty and change, overcoming evil with good. In the long run, the categorization of brothers and sisters in the Church as either political "liberals" or "conservatives" can become obnoxious, promoting division. Efforts at unity rather than division are more generally helpful.

Arguments for members in America also occur as to whether the Constitution of the United States is a conservative or liberal document. It has both characteristics, much as stated above.

The Church seeks for truth as its standard and stands for freedom of the individual, the rule of law, and justice. Section 134 of the Doctrine and Covenants sets forth a declaration of belief concerning governments and laws in general. The declaration, written in 1835, contains principles that merit constant reference in weighing speeches, policies, and pamphlets of the day.

My answer will probably leave much to be desired on the part of those who see either political conservatism or liberalism as being more important than the principles set forth in the declaration, or who attempt to steer the thinking of their ward or branch toward any current political position. But the declaration has served the Church well and continues to provide inspiration to its members. (See especially the basic principles set forth in verse 2.) —— *G. Homer Durham*

My ecology class in school
is very critical of people
who are selfish enough
to bring more than two children
into the world when it is becoming
overpopulated and so highly polluted.
How can I answer this?

To determine whether or not an act is selfish, we must know the motives and values of the persons concerned. I hope you have discussed the word *ethnocentrism* in your sociology or social science classes. Ethnocentrism is a term for the tendency of human groups to view their own values as right and proper and to view all other values or ways of doing things as incorrect, evil, or even selfish.

The phrase "people who are selfish enough to bring more than two children into the world" is a perfect example of ethnocentrism. The phrase says that obviously, anyone who could want more than two children must be selfish—and likely many other negative things as well, since he doesn't think the way the teacher or the majority of the class thinks.

Let's examine a few examples that would represent selfishness from your classmates' point of view. A governor launches a highway safety campaign to reduce accident fatalities; a physician struggles to keep elderly people alive; a nurse works to help premature or sickly children survive; a soldier takes prisoners rather than killing the helpless enemy; a social worker tries to improve hygienic conditions and thereby reduce infant mortality in a city slum.

Each example is one that expresses the value that people are important, that the sanctity of individual human life outweighs the abstraction of overpopulation.

In terms of the original question, the people in these examples are all behaving selfishly in that they are maintaining or even increasing the size of the population because of their belief in some other higher value.

Stephen Crane once wrote a poem with a line to the effect, "Think as I think . . . or you are a toad." The response was, "I will, then, be a toad." In dealing with ethnocentric persons whose favorite cause has become overpopulation, people who have higher priorities had better resign themselves to being labeled toads. But that's the burden of being different—and of having the gospel's set of values.

I am afraid there is no easy response to your question, "How can I answer this?" Simply put, you have one set of values; they have another. Our democratic societies guarantee your right to embrace values different from those of your neighbors. You have a right to your beliefs about the sanctity of human life and the beauty of children, and you have the right to have a family that allows you to express those values in your behavior.

Similarly, those who choose to prevent children from being born or who choose to severely limit their numbers, rather than learning how to organize and share in a way so that more children could be accommodated in their homes, also have a right to their values.

The fact is that there is no real correlation between pollution and population size. For decades society has ignored the problem of pollution and has done many things that maximize short-term profits but are costly in terms of long-range pollution. Whether society is willing to make the massive changes in social organization necessary to reduce pollution or even to become a nonpolluting society remains to be seen. But to blame the problem on population size is a cop-out. Pollution stems from the way the population lives, not the size of the population.

With the advent of ecology as a big issue, the antipopulation people have changed their arguments with remarkable ease. You may recall that the argument used to be that we must cut down on our population growth or starve. It was said that unless we stopped having so many children, famine awaited.

Then, when the "green revolution" in agriculture made it

clear that the earth can feed many times its present population, the starvation argument dropped into second or third place, and pollution and crowding became the familiar arguments.

In the days when improving the standard of living was seen as a virtue, parents contemplating a family often made a conscious choice between a child and some material acquisition. "Shall it be a baby or a baby grand?" was one way the problem was put. In those days it was sometimes difficult for some people to identify the values involved and to decide which was the selfish choice. Now it is much easier. The so-called experts in population and ecology have given us the go-ahead on the baby grand, assuring us with great glee that at the same time we are making a choice for the survival of humanity. What bunk! What sheer, transparent bunk!

No one knows what an optimum population is. To specify an optimum, one must have a set of values, and science cannot provide the values to be used as input in computing this kind of an optimum. For example, if you decide that one of your values is to prevent as much starvation as possible (that is, you decide that to starve is worse than to have never been born), then you arrive at a very different optimal size than if one of your values is that human life should be experienced by as many human beings as possible.

If your over-riding value is the greatest good for the greatest number, and if you spell out what is meant by "good," then you may have another optimum size.

The point is that all the talk about overpopulation is tied to assumptions about *how many* people ought to be supported, *the way* they should be supported, and *why.* But these underlying values are rarely, if ever, specified.

Sometimes persons are impressed with the rhetoric of the antipopulationists and pass that rhetoric along without realizing that its underlying values and assumptions run counter to many of their own values. Today, the notion of overpopulation is in. It is one of the most accepted ideas of our time. Few persons bother to ask what it really means or to ask which values are taken into account in deciding what is the over-, under-, or optimum population size.

But for you, a follower of Christ, the setting is somewhat different. The values that make up the gospel of Jesus Christ derive from Christ's teachings about who man is and what earth life is for. Let's make some of these values explicit. The gospel teaches that man, an eternal being, is a child of God. The gospel teaches that life is a very important period of schooling, but it is only one phase of man's existence. The gospel teaches that one of the chief reasons for coming to earth is to obtain a physical body. Receiving this body and the opportunities associated with mortal life constitute critical steps in each man's progress toward his eternal destiny. As children of God and members of an eternal race, we recognize that this mortal life is temporary and that the apparent limits here—three dimensions, death, beginnings, and endings, sorrow and pain—do not necessarily apply in existence beyond mortality.

The gospel teaches that man, a child of God, is more important than any of God's other creations. Trees, rivers, air, wilderness, earth, and even other worlds were created for man; he was not created for them. "This is my work and my glory," God states, "to bring to pass the immortality and eternal life of man." (Moses 1:39.) This does not mean that man is to treat these creations with disrespect; on the contrary, a profound reverence for all forms of life and for the miraculous, complex working of nature is one of the hallmarks of the Christian life. But our scale of priorities is clear: a human being is worth more than a tree, a forest, a national park, or even the wealth of the whole earth.

In light of these values, phrases like "baby pollution" make me shudder. The earth exists for us, not the reverse. The issue is never earth versus man, but rather earth for use of man. The priorities are clear: the benefits of earth life should be given to as many of our eternal race as possible. If earth life is a period of schooling, let us organize ourselves so that the benefits of that schooling can be had by all whom our Father wishes to send. And let us understand that the advantages of that schooling do not depend on the maintenance of any particular man-land ratio, nor the return of every family to a family farm. A place in the country and a two-car garage—or even a small apartment and access to Central Park—are not the prerequisites for a quality experience on earth.

To those persons who see man as a descendant of lower forms of life, an accident in an accidental universe, and who see life as a brief and nasty experience leading nowhere, perhaps it makes sense to try to ensure that their own and their offspring's world be as pleasant and unchallenging as possible. In this perspective, whether there be few men, many men, or no men at all is really of little consequence, and perhaps they would say the fewer men, the better.

But if we believe that man is the offspring of God, that the earth is for man, and that earth life is a time to gain a body as well as experience living with other men, then some of the so-called problems are transformed into life-giving challenges.

You must realize that in the end, unless your classmates and teachers either share your values or are willing to respect them, you cannot answer their population and ecological questions to their satisfaction. This is because your views on the nature of mankind are different from theirs—facts that you interpret one way, they will interpret another. Believe me, the differences are deep and fundamental. Perhaps, at least with your close friends, the discussions should begin at the "what is man and what can he become?" stage, rather than with your views on the population problem.

However, you should know that the problems human societies are experiencing are not due to population, *per se,* but to corrupt and inefficient forms of social organization. Some of the experts would have you believe otherwise simply because it is much easier to prevent children from being born than to convince the grown men and women of the world to change the values by which they live.

We too believe that environmental pollution is a serious problem. But it flows *not* from population size, but from societies being badly trained, poorly organized, heedless of the consequences of their actions. We believe that if you teach the human family correct principles, they can create a quality and quantity of human life on a scale now unimagined.

In closing, let me list a few quick answers. To people who lament about space, point out that most of the earth's land surface is uninhabited, or sparsely inhabited. We should stop pouring our resources into killing each other and should learn how to make the rest of the earth habitable. If that does not provide enough space—and some of the population projections are designed to impress the reader that a population of infinity is just around the corner—then talk about cities on the sea, under the sea, or towering into the sky. Given the speed that the last decade's science fiction has become this decade's fact, such notions are not too far out. Man is too culture-bound in his ideas about what kinds of living facilities humans can use. If your interrogator finds earth too small, point out that a solar system and universe out there await colonization, and that the challenge of conquering space is not likely to be met so long as earth is sparsely populated. In short, space is not the problem. Don't let anyone tell you that it is. Intelligence, imagination, and industriousness are the things in short supply.

To people who lament about food: take note of all the land we keep out of production to keep prices up and all the land we don't bother to cultivate because we lack the knowledge or the resources to make it productive, and take note of all the land that could be better used. Note also the underdeveloped state of hydroponics, farming the sea, and creation of foodstuffs in chemical laboratories. Finally, observe the tremendous waste and inefficiencies in preparation, distribution, and storage of foods. Food is not the problem. Business and international politics are the problems.

If food is not the problem, and space is not, then what? Is the problem that we don't have enough wilderness areas available? Then legislate! Organize the landmass in such a way that sufficient areas stay available. It can be done. In the end, if the choice is between having to reserve one's space in a national park two years in advance and allowing another million children to be born, I opt for the children.

So recognize the ethnocentrism—the name-calling—for what it is, and learn to live with it. Face up to some of the facts about what it means to be a follower of Christ. The Savior warned his followers that they should expect persecution. Bearing the label "selfish" for our defense of large families in an antifamily era may be one of the forms of persecution the Saints in our time will have to bear.

Finally, you should always keep it clearly in mind that the name-calling derives from a fundamental conflict of values. Don't be disturbed when you find that reconciliation within the value framework of your friends is impossible. As a Latter-day Saint, you disagree with certain people on the nature of man, so it is to be expected that you would disagree about how to deal with the problems of mankind.——*Howard M. Bahr*

I don't feel "in" with religion.
What difference does it make
if I enjoy X-rated movies and novels
of contemporary morality standards?

I suspect that many of us find it difficult to feel totally "in" with religion 100 percent of the time. True religion demands the best that is in us, and a total effort is not always easy to give. It is a very human quality that leads us to become discouraged when the requests of the religious life begin to seem excessive. For some, the problem may be the claim religion makes upon their time; for others, the problem may come in the form of personality conflicts with someone in the Church; for still others, the lure of forbidden fruit may seem almost too strong to resist. It can be difficult during the times one feels "out of it" to resist such feelings of resentment or allurement without help. However, aid has been offered by the Savior, who, with his total awareness of our problems and also of our desires to have the best in life, is perhaps the only one qualified to render assistance.

Let us consider, for example, one of the most important teachings of Jesus in connection with the problem you have suggested. I refer to his teaching concerning the power and importance of thought. Because our thoughts ultimately determine our actions, Jesus repeatedly emphasized the need for good thoughts and proper motives if one is ever to come to peace with himself. Any activity that creates improper thoughts has the potential to destroy our happiness.

It is in this context, perhaps, that we should give careful consideration to the types of amusements we seek, recognizing their potential influence on our thought. If we seek complete happiness, we must face squarely the problem created by contemporary standards in the entertainment and art media. Many of the standards employed in the creation of contemporary movies and novels, for example, are clearly antithetical to the major thrusts of the gospel, and exposure to them may be a very large part of the reason some do not feel "in" with religion. Instead, they find themselves divided and torn, desiring the good life but also being unwilling to put aside that which is directly opposed to it. They find themselves like Augustine of old, who prayed, "Lord, give me chastity, . . . only not yet, For I feared lest Thou shouldest hear me soon, and soon cure me of the disease of concupiscence, which I wished to have satisfied, rather than extinguished." (*The Confession of St. Augustine,* Book VIII.) Inner peace flees them and they find that to restore it, they must make a choice between the two.

How then, at times like these, does one find strength to give up that which he seems to enjoy so much? A partial solution to our problem, it seems to me, lies in another of the teachings of Jesus—the important truth that one can drive out bad thoughts with better thoughts. I suspect, for example, that anyone who enjoys X-rated movies and novels with contemporary morality standards would also enjoy a better quality of movie or a better novel, and both are available if one is willing to look for them. Therefore, why not decide in favor of the best within us and seek out higher forms of entertainment and instruction, thereby elevating our thoughts and ultimately our lives, letting our recreational moments become literally moments of re-creation? As Marcus Antonius remarked many centuries ago, "The happiness of your life depends upon the quality of your thought." The Master has added in our own time, "Let virtue garnish thy thoughts *unceasingly.*" (D&C 121:45. Italics added.) Ultimately this seems the only way to truly feel "in" with religion.——
Arthur R. Bassett

*Can people who build so many fences
around certain experiences, such as no smoking, no drinking,
and no immorality, ever be real artists?
Mustn't the artist almost by definition
live either totally without fences
or with only makeshift,
empirical fences-of-the-moment?*

Certainly there cannot help but be a definite correlation between the depth of a person's own experiences and his capacity to create. Therefore, you ask, mustn't the artist (actor, writer, painter) open his soul to every possible experience that will increase his firsthand awareness of all that human life encompasses?

24

I happen to believe quite truly that there is a Divine Being who is our spiritual Father by virtue of his operating through divine laws that we too must operate through if we are to fulfill the measure of our creation. For this reason I am concerned with myself first as a person and second as a potential artist. I accept Jesus Christ as being divine. But putting that aside, I consider the patterns of behavior that he taught to be the most perfect that could ever be devised for the successful living of human life. The acceptance of this gives me little choice in the kinds of things I must at least try to do with my life. If I should behave in ways that are contrary to these beliefs for the sake of enlarging my reservoir of experience, there would be a basic violation of my integrity.

However, I do not believe that in following these patterns of behavior I am losing more than I am gaining in the absorbing of significant human experiences. There is something not entirely true in the image of building fences around the experiences disapproved. One cannot partake of every possible human experience. Sometimes the experiencing of one automatically builds a fence around the experiencing of another. Holding a belief in God is a significant human experience. So is holding a disbelief in God. Many people bounce around on the edges of both, and some sincerely embrace both at different times; but no one, just at will, can experience both of these possibilities—the one builds a fence around the other.

I hope no one tries to tell me that I'm missing a significant human experience by building a fence around smoking cigarettes or drinking alcohol. The only thing of any significance this does is (when I'm away from home) to separate me in this particular thing from the group norm. And what's wrong with that? Sometimes that separation itself turns into quite an interesting experience.

The fact of the matter is that the way I construct my fences permits certain types of experiences that most people fence out entirely by not even considering. But these very experiences constitute the greater part of my own joyful probings into life. The act of prayer, I believe, is one of the most significant of human experiences. Other more material acts also qualify. The payment of tithing is an experience in giving, in trust, and in obedience that has quite an impact on the character. The act of fasting has effects that are significant. People build fences around these experiences just as I build fences around the things that I do not do. Everyone builds fences. And everyone must choose experiences. The critical point is whether the choosing is done unthinkingly, or from social pressure, or from cowardice, or from a desire to be really significant yourself.

While I was in Russia several years ago, I had an interview with the head professor of the Moscow Art Theatre School, Alexander Mehilovich Karev. In our conversation he said to me, "I once asked Stanislavsky, 'The man who kills, can he play a better Othello than the man who does not?' 'Yes,' he said; 'if he's more talented.' "——*Carol Lynn Pearson*

*How does one know
when he is becoming a fanatic
on a principle and letting things
get out of balance?*

Satan is a horizontal extremist. That is one of the chief methods he employs in fighting against God, as he tries to pervert every true and righteous concept by tempting us to become unbalanced in its application. Depending on the individual, Satan will either strive to have the concept repudiated and abandoned or carried to the opposite point of possible obsessive involvement. Thus, he would have us love too little or too much, feel remorse for sin too little or too much, be concerned about physical health too little or too much, and so forth.

Therefore, we are becoming fanatical when we exalt one principle at the expense of all others, when we become a respecter of principles by making too much of one and too little of others. We then lack spiritual symmetry; we are distorted, unbalanced, and false.

We are getting things out of balance when our commitment causes us to alienate ourselves from our fellow saints and mortals, when we find ourselves sitting in judgment on those who do not share our magnificent obsession with a certain point of view (probably on a point that has elements of speculation in it), and when we reject others because we disagree with their views.

We are out of balance and becoming fanatical when we feel a pride in our own presumed deeper comprehension of God's true will, and in an assumed spiritual superiority over our non-member brothers and sisters. We are losing perspective when, like some of the Pharisees, we care, so to speak, more about the Sabbath than man and more about some principle that supposedly divides us than about the fatherhood of God and the brotherhood of man that were meant to unite us.——*Rodney Turner*

Are certain forms of creative art discouraged in the Church, such as modern visual art and modern dance?

The tendency to categorize in an over-simplified way exists with us all. We frequently use catchall terms, such as *modern painting, classical art,* and *modern education.* As a rule these terms are so general they have little meaning, and we should be more specific in making our subject known.

Modern art is a good example. The trends in contemporary visual arts are extremely varied, ranging from modes of abstract art to super-realism (a highly realistic interpretation of subject matter), which at present is the closest thing to a current movement in the visual art world. The same broad variety of expressions now exists in all areas of the visual and performing arts. Consequently, it is impossible to evaluate modern art or modern dance in a meaningful way. One must refer not only to specific kinds of expression but also to specific artists and specific works if an evaluation is to be valid.

It is important to remember that good and bad quality exists in all forms of expression. There is good traditional art and poor traditional art. There is good modern art and poor modern art.

Works that are good—even significant in artistic accomplishments—may be offensive morally. Moral judgments can and should be made by each of us about specific works of art.

Works that are offensive are certainly discouraged by the Church, although it is seldom that an official statement is issued. It is unreasonable to expect the Church to evaluate all the art that is being produced—or to play a censoring role. We, as individuals, must be sensitive enough in these matters to recognize and shun works that are not in keeping with our beliefs and feelings. This, of course, becomes a personal judgment, and, like many aspects of our lives, it may require thoughtful introspection and the guidance of the Spirit.

There is no question that pornographic and otherwise immoral art is in great abundance today, and it is a major contribution to the worldly climate of our times. We should eschew this level of art and strive to prevent it from becoming a part of us.

At the same time we should realize there is exciting modern work being accomplished today in all fine arts areas. Modern painting, sculpture, music, theater, film, poetry, and literature are all flourishing. As spectators and participants, young people everywhere are experiencing the benefits of the arts. If we seek out and learn to appreciate the fine arts, our lives will be greatly enriched.——*Edward D. Maryon*

What are the reasons
for and the process
of excommunication?

Regaining the presence of God, the Eternal Father, is what membership in the Church is all about. Eternal life or exaltation should be the goal and objective of every Latter-day Saint. Recognizing the hazards and pitfalls of mortality and the power of the adversary to deceive and persuade in wrong directions, a kind and understanding Heavenly Father has provided a process by which we might receive the help we need to cleanse ourselves and make the necessary corrections. This pathway is commonly referred to as repentance. All of Heavenly Father's children have need of this principle in their lives from time to time. When the irregularity has been major, the church court system plays an important role in helping the transgressor find his way back. It is all for our benefit and blessing.

The bishops court and the high council court have properly been referred to as courts of love. The sole purpose of a church court is to bring about in the Lord's way a spiritual judgment for every member that will hopefully eliminate for all time an irregularity or transgression that could prevent him from the ultimate blessing of exaltation.

The Lord's plan is totally positive. His work and his glory is to provide a way whereby as many of his children as possible may return to his holy presence as family units (Moses 1:39), there to share in *all* that the Father has (D&C 84:33-39). He has no process or plan designed to block the progress of any of his children. His goal is singular; his work and his glory is that all might be edified and exalted.

The process of church court discipline might well be likened to fresh, clean water that is ever flushing out the constantly forming cesspools of sin and corruption common to mortality and continually thrust upon man by the power of Satan.

All Latter-day Saints who have need to repent must first of all find the courage to seek out their priesthood leaders for help. Relatively few transgressors are excommunicated. Some are disfellowshiped for a season; many, many more are quietly placed on probation by the bishop or stake president. The great majority of those who talk to their priesthood leaders about their personal problems are worked with confidentially without even the need for a court hearing or a formal disciplinary action. The attitude of the individual is all-important as he comes to his priesthood authority. If we seek help and correction with a contrite spirit and an unmistakable desire to do right, the priesthood leader can frequently bring about the miracle of forgiveness without the need for court action. This is particularly true of those who are in the beginning stages of transgression and those young people who have fallen prey to the adversary on a one-time or so-called experimental basis.

When excommunication is necessary, however, we must not regard the penalty as an end to all blessings and eternal possibilities. Even excommunication, serious as it is, can have the effect of restoring the proper perspective of the offender. Once a person has been deprived of church membership, it is interesting to note how vitally important rebaptism becomes. The truly repentant excommunicated person will strive diligently to regain the waters of baptism. In the Church there are scores of members who have earned their way back through true repentance and who now stand on more firm ground than ever before. They have learned their lesson well. They are not likely to make the same mistake again, and surely the blessings of eternity are once again a possibility, thanks to the sanctifying influence of true repentance coupled with the miracle of forgiveness.

A bishop has the authority to convene a bishops court. The court consists of the ward bishopric, and they may consider the matter of excommunication for any member of the Church living in the ward except one who holds the Melchizedek Priesthood. The bishops court may, however, render a decision of disfellowshipment for any member of the ward, including Melchizedek Priesthood holders. This court may also place any ward member, regardless of priesthood status, on probation.

The high council court, under the direction of the stake president, consists of the stake presidency and members of the high council. This court has the authority to conduct hearings for any member of the Church residing in the stake, including both Aaronic and Melchizedek Priesthood holders, and also the authority to impose a decision of excommunication where appropriate. Church members to be tried are notified in advance of the date, the hour, and the place the court will convene. The court should convene in the attitude of fasting and prayer. Total justice in harmony with the revealed word of the Lord should be the prime objective of the court. Judgment that is too light or too harsh often defeats the purposes of the Lord. A fair hearing and a final decision of the court that is ratified by the gifts of the Spirit will always be in the best interests of the member being tried. It is usually those who are far removed from the spirit of truth as to be imperceptive to the love of Christ and the need for proper priesthood reprimand who leave the church court with belligerence and ill feelings toward their priesthood leaders. These people are seldom sorry for what they have done but only sorry they have been caught.

Excommunication need not be the end of all hope. Although the mistake has been grievous and a serious violation of God's commandments, a person who really loves the Lord and has the desire and the fortitude to now do right can most often reestablish his life and in due process and time may possibly qualify himself for the lofty and ultimate blessings of exaltation.

There are very few reasons for excommunication in the Church. I can think of only three:

1. Church members become candidates for excommunication as they involve themselves in gross iniquity.

2. Church members become candidates for excommunication as they become involved in or advocate plural marriage.

3. Church members become candidates for excommunication as they apostatize from the teachings of the Church.

Gross iniquity involves such transgressions as murder, adultery, sexual perversion, or serious civil court conviction such as a felony.

It should also be made clear that an apostate is not an indifferent or an inactive member of the Church, but rather one who flatly denies the divine nature of the Church or one who is antagonistic against or unresponsive to his priesthood authority.

Where serious transgression requires a court hearing, may I promise you that the procedure is kind and gentle. Our court system is just; and as has been stated on many occasions, these are courts of love with the singular objective of *helping* members to get back on a proper course.——*Elder Robert L. Simpson*

What kind of emphasis should we as Latter-day Saints place on intellectual activities and pursuits?

I assume that this questioner uses the word *intellectual* to refer to such pursuits as philosophy, history, literature, the visual arts, modern and classical languages—scholarly interests that certainly *may* have a spiritual side or a practical side, but that at first glance don't seem necessarily to bear either one of these self-justifying labels. Like any question having to do with the goals of life, this problem is an important one.

I think we can justify the value of intellectual pursuits in just two words: heightened awareness. The Lord has created an endlessly fascinating world; in each place and at each period of time, his children have found an incredible variety of ways to deal with their personal and community problems and to express their discoveries, their values, and their emotions. How tragic (and dull!) for a person to know nothing beyond the limitations of his own experience—to perceive nothing but the problems, joys, and hopes of the Des Moines girl or the Inverness boy, just because that is what he or she happens to be! Education can help us to respond to feelings that lie outside our direct experience; our appreciation is refined and we become more sensitive and perceptive. The spiritual implications of this kind of growth are obvious. To learn to observe clearly, to respond compassionately, to use the lessons of other times and places to improve our own lives—surely these are some of the reasons our Heavenly Father made us thinking creatures to begin with.

Let's consider for a moment a statement by Dr. Jae R. Ballif, dean of the College of Physical and Mathematical Sciences at Brigham Young University.

"Many members of the Church make a sharp distinction between the 'religious' and the 'secular.' They often imply that the secular is less important and yet includes many broad disciplines of learning, including the sciences. As Latter-day Saints we should know better than this. Our vital task is to distinguish truth from error and pursue the truth wherever it is found. All truth, not just that encompassed by a narrow definition of the word 'religious,' can help us toward eternal salvation and toward eventual godhood. Unfortunately, many try to be godlike in their personal characteristics, but refuse to accept the responsibility for gaining knowledge and wisdom. To become like Him we must acquire His personal characteristics and His wisdom."

So intellectual pursuits *are* important. The best family member, the best genealogist, the best missionary, the best home teacher—and so on all the way down the list of our important obligations in this earthly life—is the curious person, the alive person, the person willing to expand his awareness in pursuit of "anything virtuous, lovely, or of good report, or praiseworthy"—*all* truth.

What each person must decide for himself, then, is the role that intellectual pursuits will play in his life—what scholarly matters he will pursue, when he will pursue them, or whether he will pursue them at all. But to those who reject the whole idea of intellectual pursuits, let me offer some cautions against three possible reasons for this decision that seem to me to be false ones:

1. "It won't help me earn a living." Beware of this reason! Neither will most of the important things you study in life. Equip yourself for the *ends* of life, not just the *means*. If you value only the training that will help you to earn a dollar, you are admitting that your most important goals are material ones.

2. "Girls don't need to follow intellectual pursuits." What a misconception! Our church leaders have *never* counseled that girls should be content with a second-rate education. Even if your work is centered exclusively around your home, being wise enough to know the value of intellectual pursuits can make all the difference. Be the housewife who can transform the dreaded ironing hour into the opportunity to aim one ear toward the stereo to enjoy the fine music, the play, or the language lesson that means so much to you. Be the mother who can give your children creative experiences in the arts, sciences, languages, or music, rather than the mother who rears a generation of TV watchers.

3. "People who become too smart only succeed in making themselves unhappy." Ignorance may bring one type of peace of mind but so does sedation. Brigham Young said, "Education is the power to appreciate life." Does that sound like unhappiness?

Of course, the person in pursuit of intellectual goals must arm himself with his own set of cautions. He must be energetic in his dedication. He must not use education as an excuse to postpone life and perhaps neglect his responsibilities to his family and his church. And above all, he must test each new idea for truthfulness to insure that in his case intellectual enlightenment will not be synonymous with "the pride and craftiness" of men. (See Alma 4:19.) If he diligently and prayerfully seeks after truth, he will find great joy and satisfaction as each new understanding adds to his testimony. In the eternal scheme of things, he is closer to godhood. And for the present he is a better Latter-day Saint and a more effective instrument through which our Father in heaven can bless those around him.——*Karen Lynn*

The answer is, it depends. It depends on you and your individual interests, ambitions, talents, strengths, and weaknesses. Only if your personal objectives are such that four years of college will contribute directly toward the achievement of your goals should you plan to spend four years pursuing a college degree.

Many people mistakenly believe that a four-year college degree automatically guarantees success. Consequently, many students feel unnecessary pressure to enroll in a college, with a bachelor's degree as the target. Often a two-year program (associate degree) or a technical program of one or two years' length would be much more appropriate.

Keep in mind, however, if you are interested in such professions as engineering, teaching, law, social work, medicine, and other similar fields, you will need at least four years of college—and often quite a bit more.

Each Latter-day Saint youth should take seriously the counsel of the First Presidency when they said, "The Church has long encouraged its members, and especially its youth, either to obtain a college education or to become well trained in some vocation. The positions that do not require education or training are decreasing from year to year. We, therefore, strongly urge all young people to engage and continue in formal study of some kind beyond high school. Of equal importance is the selection of an educational program that takes into account each individual's interests, talents and goals."

Regardless of the nature of the formal educational program that you pursue after secondary school, whether it be two or four or more years, the important thing is that you dedicate yourself to learning as much as possible. Learning is exciting and a lifelong experience. Remember that the glory of God is intelligence.

Elder Hugh B. Brown of the Council of the Twelve summed it up this way: "Education has always been recognized by the Church as the number one obligation of each generation to its successor and of each individual to himself. Learn and continue to learn everything possible about ourselves, our fellowmen, our universe, and our God—who is our Father."——
William R. Siddoway

Is religious education more important than academic education?

This question certainly concerns youth today. In looking toward our day, Daniel was shown when "many shall run to and fro, and knowledge shall be increased." (Daniel 12:4.)

Paul told Timothy to "study to shew thyself approved unto God, a workman that needeth not to be ashamed, rightly dividing the word of truth." (2 Timothy 2:15.) He further states, "This know also, that in the last days . . . men shall be . . . ever learning, and never able to come to the knowledge of the truth." (2 Timothy 3:1-2, 7.)

Great emphasis has been given in our time to gaining knowledge for knowledge's sake. An editorial writer for *Fortune* magazine has written: "Knowledge is no longer a thing apart from life; knowledge and education, though they remain an end in life for a few specialists, are today a means to an end, which is the enhanced understanding of everything in life."

President Joseph Fielding Smith said, "Knowledge comes both by reason and by revelation. We are expected to study and learn all we can by research and analysis. But there are limits to our learning abilities in the realms of reason and study. The things of God can be known only by the Spirit of God."

The Lord has counseled us that we should learn as much as we can about "things both in heaven and in the earth, and under the earth; things which have been, things which are, things which must shortly come to pass; things which are at home, things which are abroad; the wars and the perplexities of the nations, and the judgments which are on the land; and a knowledge also of countries and of kingdoms." (D&C 88:79.)

We must therefore conclude that we cannot neglect our academic learning if we are to follow the counsel of the Lord.

However, this does not mean that we should concentrate only on academic learning. The Lord has stated that we should "be instructed more perfectly in theory, in principle, in doctrine, in the law of the gospel, in all things that pertain unto the kingdom of God. . . ." (D&C 88:78.)

We must not believe that all academic education is separate and apart from religious education. The more knowledge we have, when obtained under the direction of the Spirit of God, the better we can understand religious teachings.

Jacob, the brother of Nephi, warned: "O the vainness, and the frailties, and the foolishness of men! When they are learned they think they are wise, and they hearken not unto the counsel of God, for they set it aside, supposing they know of themselves, wherefore, their wisdom is foolishness and it profiteth them not. And they shall perish. But to be learned is good if they hearken unto the counsels of God." (3 Nephi 9:28-29.)

The academic knowledge we gain will benefit us in our temporal pursuits, but the knowledge we gain of spiritual and eternal truths will prepare us to live happily in this life and throughout eternity in the kingdom of God.

Our eventual goal is to gain all knowledge necessary to be like our Eternal Father. We can move in that direction only if we devote our energies and abilities to gaining knowledge of God and his laws and incorporating into our lives eternal truth wherever it is found.—*J. Elliott Cameron*

Is it justifiable to borrow money for educational purposes?

For many years the General Authorities have counseled Latter-day Saints to avoid debt. In this era of easy credit and rapid proliferation of credit cards with which one can buy everything from a haircut to a color television set, the temptation to go into debt is greater than ever before. Certainly excessive personal debt can be devastating. However, Church leaders have also recognized the value of good investments and the advisability of borrowing money for legitimate reasons.

If you need to borrow for an education, here are a few principles you should keep in mind:

1. A loan should not replace personal or family responsibilities nor take the place of part-time work.

2. Borrow no more than absolutely necessary.

3. Attempt to procure a loan at the lowest interest rate available.

Many financial institutions operate through colleges and universities. There are also private and public funds designed

36

specifically to help students in need. Some loans for education are interest-free for a few months and then have a low interest rate afterwards. For more information about what is available, check with the office of student financial aid at the school, college, or university you wish to attend.

Naturally a person should do all he can to procure his education on a pay-as-you-go basis. However, if this is impossible, an individual who cannot afford the immediate costs of education may be wise to obtain a loan, if it means the difference between completing the training or not. For students in the United States, for example, studies show that it is not uncommon that the return on an investment in education beyond high school could enable one to receive at least $200,000 in additional income during a lifetime of work. In anyone's book that's a good return for one's time, effort, and money.——
Joe J. Christensen

*Because we believe in
the principle of service,
shouldn't a Latter-day Saint
orient his vocation more to
the field of public service?*

Faithful members of the Church should try to govern all aspects and facets of their lives in accordance with gospel principles, and all of their major decisions should be made with reference to those principles. This would also be true with respect to their choice of a vocation. We should not select a vocation that would involve goods or services clearly in violation of those principles; we should choose a vocation consistent with those principles.

Within the framework of principles, however, there are many possibilities for the expression of preference. One should select his vocation on that basis. Preference should involve not only what one thinks he would like to do, but that which by disposition, talent, preparation, and qualification he is likely to do successfully.

Not every person is particularly disposed toward or especially suited to those occupations usually thought of as public service. Teachers, medical people, lawyers, merchants, civic workers, and many others offer services that are obviously indispensable; but in our interrelated, interdependent society, countless other vocational and professional pursuits are equally, if not so obviously, indispensable. The researcher who perfects the vaccine and the physician who diagnoses its need and administers it are both vital contributors, and so are the technicians, distributors, salesmen, and others involved.

Any honest work involving goods or services consistent with principles of decency and integrity would seem to be acceptable for a Latter-day Saint. Much help is presently available in determining our individual capacities and predilections with respect to various types of vocations. Multitudes of diverse employment opportunities exist; new ones are constantly coming into existence, and excellent preparation and training opportunities are available. One who desires help in selecting a vocation would be wise to make use of testing and counseling services, seek advice from persons of experience and wisdom, and invoke the help of the Lord in choosing and confirming a course to follow. Good preparation, ambition, determination to give one's best, and good hard work will then lead to success in the undertaking one chooses.

Within the framework of gospel principles, selection of a vocation would seem to be a matter of individual disposition, inherent capacity, and preference.——*Elder Marion D. Hanks*

When does a missionary
receive the keys for his ministry—
when he is ordained an elder,
when he is set apart for his mission,
or when he receives his endowment?

The receipt of a missionary call from the president of the Church opens the door for the reception of the keys of that assignment. When a missionary is set apart, he receives the keys to act in his assignment. The keys are the right to "enjoy the blessing of communication with the heavens, and the privilege and authority to administer in the ordinances of the gospel of Jesus Christ, to preach the gospel of repentance, and of baptism by immersion for the remission of sins." (Joseph F. Smith, *Gospel Doctrine,* p. 142.)

The Lord tells us in Doctrine and Covenants 42:11: "Again I say unto you, that it shall not be given to any one to go forth to preach my gospel, or to build up my church, except he be ordained by some one who has authority. . . ."

The priesthood is the authority given to man to act for God. "Every man ordained to any degree of the Priesthood, has this authority delegated to him. But it is necessary that every act performed under this authority shall be done at the proper time and place, in the proper way, and after the proper order. The power of directing these labors constitutes the keys of the Priesthood. In their fulness, the keys are held by only one person at a time, the prophet and president of the Church." (Joseph F. Smith, *Gospel Doctrine,* p. 136.)

Today President Spencer W. Kimball holds all the keys of the kingdom, which gives to him the power, right, and authority to preside over the kingdom of God on earth (the Church) and to direct all of its affairs. He has delegated some of his keys to the stake president and the mission president. They, in turn, as they set a missionary apart in behalf of President Kimball, bestow upon him the keys to act in his missionary assignment.——*J. Murray Rawson*

How is the missionary's
place of assignment determined?

"We believe that a man must be called of God, by prophecy, and by the laying on of hands, by those who are in authority to preach the Gospel and administer in the ordinances thereof."

In accordance with this policy, each missionary is called of God through the president of the Church. This is the way Aaron received his call. Moses, the Lord's prophet, gave him the call from the Lord.

In the assigning of missionaries, there are numerous factors to be considered, the chief one being the inspiration received by the Missionary Executive Committee. Members of this committee review carefully and prayerfully all of the recommendations sent to them by the stakes and missions. As they make recommendations, they consider such factors as worthiness, age, experience, military status, home finances, health, language ability, desires, quotas, limitations of countries, requests, nationality, general attitudes, and the needs of the various missions. When all these factors have been duly weighed, a sincere effort is made to ascertain where the person can make the greatest contribution, and the inspiration of the Lord is earnestly sought. The tentative assignment is made subject to approval by the president of the Church, who then signs the call and has it mailed to the prospective missionary.——*President Spencer W. Kimball*

When should a young man not *go on a mission?*

In the first place, a young man does not initiate his missionary call. In light of this, it is not his prerogative to choose or not to choose to go on a mission. His bishop and stake president recommend him, and he may state his desires to them. The call comes from the president of the Church, and the young man may then accept it or reject it.

There are circumstances under which he should frankly tell his bishop that he should not be considered for a mission. If he feels himself unworthy to represent the Church as a missionary because of immorality or failure to live other Church standards, he must candidly tell his bishop.

If he has health problems, either physical or mental, that would make it difficult or impossible for him to stand the rigors of missionary service, he should advise the bishop.

He may be seriously in debt or have other financial problems that would make it inadvisable for him to go at a particular time. He should candidly counsel with his bishop on these matters.

Furthermore, if he has a critical attitude concerning the Church, if he is unwilling to go unselfishly where he is called and devote himself wholeheartedly to the work, there may be a serious question as to whether he should be considered for missionary service.

On the other hand, he should know that if he responds to a call given him and devotes himself to the work in the right spirit and attitude, walking in obedience to the counsel of those placed over him, he will come to know a joy and satisfaction such as he is not likely to experience in any other activity in life.——*Elder Gordon B. Hinckley*

Is it advisable to wait for a missionary?

This question is a difficult one to answer, because the decision as to whether or not one waits for a missionary is a personal matter and must be determined by the people involved. However, some of the following matters might be taken into consideration.

To begin with, no formal poll has been taken that I am aware of, but it appears more often than not that an agreement to wait somehow gets sidetracked during the mission, and as a result, the familiar "Dear John" letter is received by the missionary.

Any two people, especially those of the typical missionary age, change over a period of eighteen months to two years. The special nature of missionary service, of course, causes the missionary to change, but the person at home changes also. Sometimes these changes are rather dramatic on both sides, creating a situation in which a young couple almost need to become reacquainted following missionary service.

In light of this, several questions could well be asked: Will waiting be good for the person at home during the time when dating and social activity should be a prime part of a young person's life? Is it appropriate for a young person to avoid such associations for an extended period of time? Will waiting be

good for the missionary? Does having someone waiting at home 41
cause the missionary to become preoccupied with thoughts of
him or her? In order to be successful, a missionary must serve
the Lord with all his heart, might, mind, and strength. Does the
person who is waiting encourage that kind of loyalty to the
Lord, or does he or she unwittingly cause a division of loyalty?
Will waiting be good for the missionary work? If the missionary
suffers, then the work suffers. Certainly every Church member
will want to do all within his power to help missionary work
succeed, and the way it succeeds is for the missionary to succeed.

If a relationship can be mature and well-founded enough to
take into account the above points, then waiting for a
missionary might be good both for the work and for the parties
concerned. Communication should be limited to a weekly letter
and an occasional package from home. The tone of the letter
should be uplifting and encouraging. Some missionaries have
told us that sending tapes can cause problems. To actually hear
the voice of a loved one may lead to feelings of homesickness
and cause the missionary to become diverted from his work. For
the same reason it is recommended that family and friends
should not telephone the missionary in the field except in dire
emergencies, and generally only with the permission of the
mission president.——*Elder Loren C. Dunn*

Should girls go on missions?

This involves two questions: Would the mission be good for
the girl, and would the girl be good for the mission?

The answer to the first question is almost universally yes.
Nearly any girl with a positive attitude and a desire to serve will
benefit greatly from mission service. She can build her testimony, firm up her direction in life, develop a spirit of tolerance
and love, build self-confidence and a positive attitude, come to
an appreciation of home, parents, and family, and see more
clearly the importance of choosing a husband who will go with
her not only to the temple but also to the celestial kingdom.
She will feel the joy and satisfaction that comes from unselfish,
full-time service to others.

Would the girl be good for the mission?

This question cannot be answered in a general way. It's an individual matter. Today's typical lady missionary is an energetic, young (usually just turned twenty-one), enthusiastic girl who will, traditionally, participate in about twice as many conversions as will the average elder. She is usually in the mission field because she has a desire to serve, not because she is compelled by social pressure.

A girl who enters the mission field to find a solution to her personal problems is likely to feel very out of place in such company. The vigorous schedule of the mission field affords little time or place for eccentric behavior or personal problem solving.

On the subject of girls and missions, I consulted my board of advisers—three of my children: Leola (an adopted daughter), who served in the North Carolina-Virginia Mission; Roger, who served in the Washington Mission; and Greg, a missionary in California. Here are their capsule comments:

Leola: "There are certain people who are more approachable and more responsive to sisters. We found this especially true in military areas where the husband is away and the wife usually will not let men into her home."

Roger: "The lady missionaries in our mission were hardworking, conscientious, and always cheerful."

Greg: "There isn't much time to write; I've got to run. I'm tired! Why? Because we worked with the sisters today, and they worked us into the ground. Sisters surely 'spark' the zone."

Greg suggested reading the fourth section of the Doctrine and Covenants as an aid to making a decision about missionary service: "Therefore, if ye have desires to serve God ye are called to the work."

Note the two requirements: *desire* and *commitment.* It is the desire to serve God that should motivate a sister (or an elder) to accept a mission call. If the desire to serve is strong enough, the missionary will understand that it is a 100 percent commitment to "see that ye serve him with all your heart, might, mind and strength." (D&C 4:2.) If your heart isn't in it, there is little reason to put your physical self in it. It is that 100 percent commitment that makes missionary service a happy, productive experience. Without that commitment, it can be a long, miserable time.

And the rewards? ". . . he that thrusteth in his sickle with his might, the same layeth up in store that he perisheth not, but bringeth salvation to his soul." (D&C 4:4.) ". . . great shall be your joy with him [the convert you helped to influence] in the kingdom of my Father!" (D&C 18:15.) —— *Arthur S. Anderson*

Is it right to stress marriage right after a mission?

*T*his question undoubtedly refers to counsel sometimes given by well-meaning persons to missionaries—counsel that they should be married shortly after they return from their full-time missions. As a beginning point in finding an answer to this question, an investigation through the Church Historian's Office failed to locate such counsel in the speeches and writings of the presidents of the Church. However, President Joseph F. Smith did make an interesting statement on this subject. He said, "We hold that no man who is marriageable is fully living his religion who remains unmarried." (*Juvenile Instructor* 37:400.)

President Smith's statement poses the question, When is a young man marriageable? Certainly age is only one factor. The Lord expects him to be able to truly stand at the head of his family and be accountable for its economic, emotional, and spiritual welfare. The ability to do this depends upon not only age, but also total readiness for marriage. A young man must think of the training and education he will need to properly sustain his family. His financial circumstances or those of his family will determine whether he can marry and also acquire the training he needs to provide his new family with the necessities of life.

But beyond vocational and economic considerations, there is the vital question of whether he is properly prepared through an adequate courtship and engagement period.

Marriage, in the best sense of the word, is more than a legal or temple ceremony. It is a spiritual and emotional union that needs to be achieved before legal and physical union takes place. Many varied social and religious reactions and interactions must be experienced before a true oneness of spirit and personality is realized. Such a union takes time. This is especially true of dedicated Latter-day Saint youths, whose courtship might well be termed a "temple courtship."

Whereas an ordinary courtship may merely be an unplanned continuation of a dating relationship that has proven very enjoyable, a temple courtship has a unique spiritual goal—finding a suitable mate for an eternal partnership with God. It takes more time for such a courtship to reach its fruition. There must be a revelation to each other of innermost ideals and loyalties. Such a courtship involves extensive contact in a wide range of life experiences with each other's parents, relatives, and friends. Emphasis on proper preparation and readiness, and not on immediate marriage at the close of a mission, is the proper stress for the returned missionary who wants to do all he can to lay a good foundation for an eternal family kingdom.——*Ernest L. Eberhard, Jr.*

*How does the principle
of presidency work
in Aaronic Priesthood quorums?*

In a recent ward fast and testimony meeting a deacons quorum president bore his testimony from the pulpit. As he looked down to the front row of the chapel where his fellow quorum members sat, he was overwhelmed with the knowledge that he was responsible for every deacon in the ward. He exclaimed, "I just can't believe that all of you guys are really mine!"

This fine young quorum president realized that he had been called by the Lord, through the bishop, to lead his quorum members, that he was responsible to represent the Lord and to see that the Lord's will was done in the quorum. He was beginning to understand what the Savior meant when he declared: "And again, verily I say unto you, the duty of a president over the office of a deacon is to preside over twelve deacons, to sit in council with them, and to teach them their duty, edifying one another, as it is given according to the covenants." (D&C 107:85.)

There are three main phrases in that revelation that every quorum president needs to understand and apply in meeting the responsibility of his stewardship:

1. *To preside.* This means to supervise, direct, guide, or control. The quorum president holds the keys to guide his quorum so its members can fulfill their priesthood duties. He, as well as the quorum adviser, is entitled to revelation in directing that quorum, and when he does not exercise those keys, the quorum is deprived of those special blessings that can come only through their president.

2. *To sit in council with them.* This requires the quorum president to show loving concern for each quorum member, to be a friend to everyone and sensitive to individual and group needs, to direct and encourage and counsel members to be faithful to their callings, live clean lives, and honor their priesthood. The quorum president should realize that the Lord has placed the quorum membership under his leadership, and he expects the president "to sit in council with them" whenever they need his guidance and direction.

3. *To teach them their duty.* This is a challenging responsibility for a quorum president who is of the same age as the members of his quorum. But we should never forget that the Lord gave the assignment that every Aaronic Priesthood bearer is to receive instruction from the quorum president on his duties in the priesthood. The fact that others, such as the adviser, may also teach these duties does not relieve the president of his responsibility.

It is interesting to note that the Lord gave the same instructions to the presidents of the teachers and priests quorums as well as to presidents of elders quorums. That is how important he feels this counsel is.

Every Aaronic Priesthood quorum president should remember that he acts under the direction of his bishop, who is the president of the Aaronic Priesthood of the ward and is also the president of the priests quorum. In this respect, the priests quorum has unique leadership. Since the bishop is the president of that quorum, a priest cannot preside in a quorum meeting. He may conduct the meeting, but the right and responsibility to preside over the priests rests only with the bishop, and he is not authorized to delegate that right to others. He selects a priests group leader to assist him in leading the priests quorum. This young man plays a vital role in the youth programs of the ward, serving as chairman of the bishop's youth committee and leading in the activity program of the Aaronic Priesthood.

Quorum presidents are given counselors to assist them. The wise president will use his counselors effectively, counseling with them and permitting them to carry their full share of the presidency. He will meet with them regularly to plan, organize, and evaluate their performance. He will permit his counselors to take turns in conducting quorum meetings and will take them with him in visiting quorum members. The presidency should work as a team, setting the example for the quorum and providing united leadership. It is important for the quorum president to learn how to use his counselors and for them to learn how to use their president.

You who are called to be quorum presidents have a special opportunity to discover the great blessings that come through service to your fellowmen and to prepare yourselves for greater responsibilities to come. You will understand that selfishness has no place in leadership. You will realize that The Church of Jesus Christ of Latter-day Saints is organized love. You will learn to love and care about others as you meet your responsibilities. A dedicated quorum president reported that even his prayers had changed. He found himself praying for the members of his quorum instead of for his own selfish interests.

When you care enough, you will search for ways to be successful in your calling, seeking help from adult leaders, from your counselors, from personal study of the scriptures and other good books, and from your personal prayers and fasting. You will discover that every leader in The Church of Jesus Christ of Latter-day Saints has a flock to lead and, at the same time, a leader to whom he is responsible—even the prophet. The effective quorum president will sustain and follow his leaders as he expects his quorum to follow him. He will also develop his "flock" by delegating responsibilities to them so they can develop leadership qualities and share the blessing of involvement.

Above all, remember that you have been called by the Lord, through his servants. He has promised everyone who has leadership responsibilities in his kingdom that when the leader does his best to fulfill his assignment, the Lord will enlarge his capacity to serve, strengthen his testimony, overcome his weaknesses, and bless the lives of those he is called to lead. Follow the example of Nephi, who, with unwavering faith, responded to

the Lord's call to accomplish a difficult task: "I will go and do the things which the Lord hath commanded, for I know that the Lord giveth no commandments unto the children of men, save he shall prepare a way for them that they may accomplish the thing which he commandeth them." (1 Nephi 3:7.)——
Robert L. Backman

*How can I get my parents
to understand that I feel different
than they do about some things?*

Generally speaking, parents and children always have had and will likely continue to have different points of view on certain matters. But please remember that your parents know this. It does not have to be brought to their attention. When significant differences come up, the question we need to ask is, How can these few differences best be resolved for the good of all concerned?

Some differences may arise because parents can see the slippery, rocky, and faintly marked sections of the road that perhaps you cannot see. It has been impressive to me to see how members of each generation, when they are grown, express strong gratitude for the wise counsel and guidance of their parents—yet it was this guidance that seemed so restrictive only a few years earlier.

Occasionally, when serious differences of opinion exist, parents and youths might ask themselves, What is right from the Lord's point of view? It might help for you to be acquainted with the advice given to parents by the Lord in Doctrine and Covenants 68:28: "And they shall also teach their children to pray, and to walk uprightly before the Lord." This is a commandment to parents, "or the sin [will] be upon the heads of the parents." (D&C 68:25.)

If your differences come because you are deviating from the teachings and practices of the gospel, conscientious parents will feel keenly about pointing this out to you. The problem then becomes not one of disagreement with your earthly parents, but one of disagreement with your Heavenly Father and Jesus Christ.

48

Here are some ways to positively and happily resolve differences of opinion in a family.

1. With a desire to learn the Lord's will, pray sincerely that the Holy Ghost may assist you in reaching a solution that is good.

2. Enter wholeheartedly into family home evening in your home, where opportunity is given for each member of the family to express himself in a spirit of constructive comment.

3. If other kinds of differences suggest discussion at other times, bring them up when your family is in a period of peace, goodwill, and happiness.

4. Be sure your differences are more than molehills—items that are only temporarily important. Don't destroy the love you have for each other over matters that likely will not be very important to you ten years from now.

5. Keep your discussions low-key, and don't wait until you are angry and upset.

6. Listen to your parents. Hear them out; then ask them to hear you out. But remember that sometimes parents and youth talk too much about their problems. Silence properly used is golden.

7. Let your parents think over your point of view. You shouldn't ask them to make hasty, ill-advised decisions.

8. When all else fails, be patient. Remember that "this too shall pass." If you really do feel like rejecting their counsel, weigh and examine your own conclusions. I've always found it wise to take each reason I think is a good one on my side and ask if it really holds up. And sometimes it doesn't. You'll probably find this same thing true when you examine some of your reasons.

One last thing: My answer here is to a question about the *differences* that exist. It's always easy to see or sense some of these differences, but don't forget all that you hold in *agreement* with your parents—the gospel, your love for each other, many good experiences, countless choice times together, many memories, many sacrifices, common beliefs and ideals on many matters. When you add it all up, you'll be amazed at how much you and your parents agree upon. It would be so foolish to take a difference that may represent only 1 percent of your total contact with your parents and blow it up out of proportion, especially when you agree on the remaining 99 percent. How sad that some young people have done this and have destroyed

their relationship with those who are really their best friends, *49*
especially in a day when real, honest, and eternally true friends
are hard to come by.——*Ernest L. Eberhard, Jr.*

*To whom should we go
for help with our problems,
particularly those dealing
with use of drugs?*

There should be no member of the Church who cannot receive help if he or she sincerely wants it. In the Church we have three main sources of help: the Savior, Church members, and our own family.

The Savior and his love are as near and as real as we permit. His presence and that of the Holy Spirit will carry us through the darkest of hours if we are open and humble. At the same time he will respect our free agency and will stay away if we reject him. In our very materialistic world I fear that many of us, even in the Church, do not accept the Savior as a practical source of help. We are far too used to material things and to so-called experts who say they can solve our problems, whether they include a broken television set or a broken life.

The Lord's church is an organized, orderly group of people who, when they follow the Lord's servants, can bring almost limitless amounts of skill, experience, and love to bear upon a problem. And our family, which includes people beyond our immediate relatives, is also a rich reservoir of help.

The Social Services Department of the Church has long felt that the solution to drug abuse among Latter-day Saints lies in reaffirmation of gospel truth in the life of the drug user. Final and lasting cure of drug use is rarely, if ever, seen unless the individual changes his behavior quite markedly. The Latter-day Saint who is on drugs may have some very understandable reasons for his behavior, but he has no excuse. In most cases drug abuse is related to loneliness, deep self-doubt, frustration with the more depressing pressures of life, and occasionally foolish experimentation with so-called friends. Even so, the one specific step into or out of drug usage occurs when a person chooses to take or not to take a drug.

Of course, we all need help and need it often. When we are in the depths of sin or have strayed far from the protection of the Lord's community, we need help more than ever. Every bishop or branch president should be able, through his welfare services committee, to contact someone who can help with a drug problem. The key steps are identifying the extent of use or abuse, the behavior behind the drug involvement, and the most appropriate course of treatment.

Obviously, if a person is addicted, especially to hard drugs like heroin, careful medically supervised detoxification or withdrawal is necessary. At the same time, the social and emotional problems leading to drug use must be identified and changes made. To help with this, the bishop can call upon qualified members of the ward, stake, or region or call in the Church social service worker assigned to his region. All this should be done confidentially through the welfare services program over which the bishop presides in his ward. We have seen success in certain parts of the Church with small, priesthood-led groups where drug users work through their problems and at the same time rebuild their relationship with the gospel.

When the medical-physical situation is under control, longer-range help can be given by a reliable, mature friend. It would be a challenging and appropriate home teaching assignment for a qualified priesthood brother to be asked to be with and strengthen a brother or sister through the ups and downs of recovery from drug use.

Finally, may I just comment on the importance of reading the scriptures and praying. Without doubt, one of the most powerful weapons in the lonely struggle against drugs is a true friend. At the same time there is also power in our spiritual relationship with the truths found in the scriptures. The Savior knows us and he knows our sufferings. His own suffering far exceeded anything we can imagine, and his compassion also exceeds anything we can imagine. When he says something, he speaks the truth.

In this regard, two of his statements are very pertinent. He said, "And I now give unto you a commandment to beware concerning yourselves, to give diligent heed to the words of eternal life. For you shall live by every word that proceedeth forth from the mouth of God. For the word of the Lord is truth, and whatsoever is truth is light, and whatsoever is light is Spirit, even the Spirit of Jesus Christ." (D&C 84:43-45.) He also said, "And ye shall know the truth, and the truth shall make you free." (John 8:32.)

Prayer and study of the scriptures are far more than a mental experience. When done with hope and faith, they become an exciting, powerful journey toward dignity, self-confidence, and power over all temptation and weakness.

Now, I have been deeply involved in the drug scene as one who attempts to help. When you say "hell," you describe it accurately. I realize that it is not enough, usually, just to study and pray. One of the most pressing duties of the Church Social Services is to help our bishops, and all members, become sensitive to the needs we all have for help and friendship all the time and special help in special times of need.

The Savior has strongly pointed out our need for the comfort and help only a friend can give. Father Lehi's words seem to summarize it well: "But behold, the Lord hath redeemed my soul from hell; I have beheld his glory, and I am encircled about eternally in the arms of his love." (2 Nephi 1:15.) ——*Victor L. Brown, Jr.*

How should we deal with friends who are taking drugs? How can we help them?

Be wisely cautious but loving. Perhaps this sounds confusing, but the drug scene is both dangerous and confusing.

There is a difference between drug experimentation and drug abuse. Many young people today tamper with drugs, which is foolish but usually temporary. Others go much further and become addicted both to the drug and to the culture of drug users.

You can help them most by setting an example of strong, healthy, Christian living. The central figure of Christianity is Jesus Christ, who loved all of us. You can demonstrate love

52 without judging and without condemning the tragedy of improper drug use.

Some specific suggestions might be:

✳ 1. Look for the better qualities in your associates. Don't condemn them because they dress differently or have unusual ideas.

2. Demonstrate in your own life the rewards of righteous living, such as good health, happiness, peace, and accomplishment.

✳3. Never agree with the improper use of drugs. Speak against it firmly and intelligently.

4. Do not attempt to "treat" drug abusers. Encourage them to go to someone who knows how to help, such as their bishop, doctor, or school counselor.

5. Remember that drug use and abuse are symptoms of the unrest and confusion in our world. Stronger families, moral living, better education, and a more Christlike society are the solutions to the drug crisis.

6. The drug abuser, the one who is addicted, often supports his habit by theft or robbery or other illegal means. Do not get trapped by unwise involvement in this type of behavior.

7. Be very cautious with drug abusers, because they often lie with great skill. They have had to learn this to cover up their habit.

The drug user or the drug abuser is a child of our Father in heaven. Consequently, he is to be loved, not rejected. He has his free agency, which means that you can help only up to the point where he must take over and change on his own. If he does not want to change, there is little you can do. If he does want to change, then your consistent and intelligent love, interest, and support may make the difference between his success and his failure.——*Victor L. Brown, Jr.*

Why can't I date when I am fifteen? I have nonmember friends who are permitted to date at this same age.

As I have listened to the counsel of the Brethren through the years, there seems to be a general sentiment among them that dating, on a one-boy-with-one-girl basis, should be postponed

until the mid to late teens and that going steady should be a
part of only marriageable-age dating.

Elder Mark E. Petersen has said that early dating often leads to early and unsuccessful marriage. President David O. McKay said, "Going steady too young oftentimes leads to intimacies which are encouraged by dating with one partner only."

The pamphlet *For the Strength of Youth,* which is endorsed by the First Presidency, counsels, "When young people enter senior high school (approximately Laurel-priest age), they may appropriately date with the consent of their parents, who are the best judges as to whether they are mature and responsible enough for this kind of young adult experience."

May I give my personal feelings on this matter. We have six sons, and we decided not to permit them to date on a one-boy-one-girl basis until they are sixteen.

I recently talked to a stake director of Young Women who remarked that a great deal of mental maturing occurs between fifteen and a half and sixteen and that she certainly could see the wisdom of a person waiting until sixteen to date. I think President Kimball gives us strong direction in this. In a talk titled "Save the Youth of Zion," delivered in 1965 at June Conference, he said, "Early dating, especially early steady dating, brings numerous problems, much heartache, and numerous disasters. The early date often develops into the steady date, and the steady date frequently brings on early marriage, of which there are hundreds of thousands with 16- and 17-year-old brides. Early marriages often end in disillusionment, frustration, and divorce, with broken homes and scarred lives. Far more high school marriages end in divorce than marriages of more mature young people. Dating, and especially steady dating, in the early teens is most hazardous. It distorts the whole picture of life. It deprives the youth of worthwhile and rich experiences. It limits friendships and reduces acquaintances which can be so valuable in selecting a partner for time and eternity."

In my own experience I will recall a mother who visited her bishop. She said, "We have given my daughter permission to date, and she is just fifteen. She is more mature than other girls her age." Physically she was more mature than other girls her age, and the mother felt totally justified in letting this young lady date. Of course, the bishop counseled very strongly against it, but to no avail. Within a short time the daughter came in alone to see the bishop, heartbroken and carrying a burden of

54

guilt that a person so young—any person, in fact—should never have to carry.

How foolish we are to suppose that when the prophets speak we may choose to ignore their counsel and advice and to make decisions contrary to theirs. My personal counsel to our youth would be to follow the prophet, obey his counsel, walk in the footsteps he would have you follow, and remain clean and pure. In due time you will have the opportunity to date, and at that time, hopefully, you will be mentally mature and able to handle the new emotions and feelings that swell inside the normal young person's physical body. The odds for remaining clean and pure and going worthily to the sacred altars in the temple, never having transgressed the moral code, very much favor those who do not date until they are sixteen.

Now, my dear young friends, the Lord doesn't always tell us why. We simply get direction and sometimes have to trust. Often your parents will not be able to tell you why they feel you shouldn't date until you are sixteen; the bishop cannot give you all the reasons. All they know is that they feel at peace in their heart with this decision, and that is probably the greatest answer that can be given. Follow their counsel, obey them, and know that the decisions you make in this very serious matter will have eternal implications.

Satan is desirous of destroying every young person in the Church and frustrating God's work. This will not happen, for our youth have been given a clear signal. We are confident that as you mature and grow in the gospel you will come to anchor your souls to the Savior. You will find strength beyond anything you have ever known. There will never be a temptation come to you that will be too great to bear. There will always be a way to escape. God will watch over you and bless you. Trust in him, be prayerful, study the scriptures, attend your meetings regularly, and choose your friends wisely. Make this a matter of great and significant prayer.

My young friends, all I can say to you is, I feel at peace with this decision in my home. Each family head must make the decision. The Church will not make it. We only offer guidelines. God bless you always and keep you clean and pure.—*Elder Vaughn J. Featherstone*

Should a young girl date boys
who are not members of the Church
if she lives in a small branch
or ward where there are few
or no Latter-day Saint boys?

Dating implies acceptance by one's peers and helps one to gain not only friends but also confidence. From personal experience with our daughters who lived in an area where there were not many Latter-day Saint boys, I know the feelings and reasons behind such a question.

But in this matter, each girl's own standard of conduct and her long-term goals are of prime importance. To be married in the temple of our Lord is an aspiration of the highest priority for Latter-day Saint girls, and thus your dating ultimately revolves around the way you can make your dream a reality.

In every relationship, one receives and gives. The standards to which a girl adheres will be honored by her date and will influence his own thinking and conduct. As followers of Christ, we are to be in the world but not of it, and it is important that those around us are aware of our conduct and principles.——
Lenore Romney

Should we pray with our dates
before going out,
while we are out on a date,
or when we come home?

Whenever prayer is offered with a sincere heart in a reverential, worshipful manner, it is appropriate. As you seriously consider the intent of your prayer, you will become aware of those circumstances most suited to communication with your Father in heaven.

Further questions concerning when one should pray could be asked to help you find your own right answer. What is the intent and purpose of having prayer with a date? Just because it seems like a good habit? To strengthen a boy-girl relationship that is very special? A request for protection in relation to travel? A personal yearning to be more confident, with ability to speak more freely? It may be a request to be endowed with the power to resist and avoid all temptation and be protected from the adversary, or maybe to comply with the words spoken by President N. Eldon Tanner, to "remember who you are and act accordingly."

If, however, the only reason is to let your date know you are a "righteous" person, there are other ways of sharing your testimony and commitment that may be even more effective. Consistently high standards will speak loudly in your behalf. You reveal your spirituality and your faith in your attitude, your speech, and your conduct.

Whenever a prayer is offered on a date, whether kneeling in your home or in the mountains, the important thing is to have faith and be in tune so that after your prayer is offered you are prepared to listen for and expect an answer. The Lord has directed his children to pray "always that they faint not; and inasmuch as they do this, I will be with them even unto the end." (D&C 75:11.) He has further instructed us, "Pray always, that you may come off conqueror; yea, that you may conquer Satan, and that you may escape the hands of the servants of Satan that do uphold his work." (D&C 10:5.)

As we think about praying with friends, we should know that the Lord has said, ". . . you must pray vocally before the world as well as in secret, and in your family, and among your friends, and in all places." (D&C 23:6.)

Anticipation of a date brings with it some unknowns. Life is a path untraveled, and hurdles can loom across one's way unexpectedly. Situations may come that you are not prepared to handle. Having committed yourself to your Father in heaven to do the best you can, you may request added strength and protection for situations you may not be able to handle alone, such as discouragement, disappointment, and danger, as well as in all other temptations found in the many vile winds that are blowing to thwart your progress and distract you from the path that will lead you to your ultimate destination.

As you choose to make prayer a vital part of your daily life, you are opening the door or responding to the invitation to establish that relationship, that communication, that powerline with God, who knows you and knows your needs and the yearnings of your heart even before you pray. ". . . for your Father knoweth what things ye have need of, before ye ask him." (Matthew 6:8.)

In preparation for a date or any other occasion, there is a strength and feeling of protection and well-being that comes from a very personal private communication addressed to the Father and in the name of Jesus Christ. As we learn to listen for those promptings of the Spirit in answer to our prayers, we draw strength from communication with our Heavenly Father.

Young people who are conscientious about their private prayers and then come together for a date can be sure they will each bring to that association a sweet spirit and influence.

A prayer together before, during, or after a date is not usually necessary, and in some cases could cause misunderstanding or embarrassment if both parties do not share the same regard for such an experience. And it is well to note that prayers on the occasion of a date are worthless if, following the prayer, you deliberately allow yourselves to be found in situations where the Spirit of the Lord will not be present. These prayers become a mockery to God, and God will not be mocked. (D&C 104:6.)

Many wonderful friendships grow out of the dating years, and young men and young women have a powerful influence on each other for good or ill. Association with a boy or girl who has private prayers regularly and strives to live accordingly is a strength to all who share the influence of that friendship. At that time when two people begin to think seriously of each other and the possibility of planning an eternal companionship develops, then the need to learn to pray together and unitedly supplicate the Lord is essential. It is this awareness of each other's spiritual potential and relationship with the Savior that reveals the most important attributes required of one who may become your eternal companion.

As you seek earnestly for direction, you will want to remember the admonition given in the Doctrine and Covenants: "Be thou humble; and the Lord thy God shall lead thee by the hand, and give thee answer to thy prayers." (D&C 112:10.) ——
Ardeth G. Kapp

What standards should I have in dating?
Am I expected to show affection
for a girl on our first date,
such as putting my arm around her?
What is the proper thing to do?

Before sitting down to write this answer, I took occasion to ask several attractive young girls how they would respond to this question. Without exception, each indicated in her own way that a boy should feel no responsibility to put his arm around a girl to show her some affection. One of the girls said, "Boys who try to do that really lose points with me."

Afterwards, each took some time to respond to other aspects of this rather complex question. One young lady said that she greatly admired young men who knew how to be courteous, doing such things as being on time, walking on the outside down the street, being responsive to parents' requests about when they would like their daughter to be home, knowing when the girl or the boy should go first, opening car doors, and being genuine in conversation.

Perhaps one of the most important points mentioned was that the question seemed to imply that a person should have one set of standards for ordinary living and another for dating. The girls' point of view is that we should have one consistent set of high standards in our lives; thus, we would avoid the problem of trying to decide which set of standards we should be applying at any given time.

Almost everyone desires to find, at the appropriate time, a companion who is warm, considerate, and affectionate. In life, at appropriate times and in appropriate ways, we all need to experience the feeling of being loved. Holding someone's hand and putting one's arm around another can be meaningful experiences if the setting, timing, and relationship are right.

But there are times when some young people treat the sharing of physical affection in dating much like a game, which they attempt to play on every date. They fail to understand that although the sharing of physical affection is an important part of a wholesome married relationship, it is not the most important. In some ways, physical affection is to marriage as seasoning is to a meal. Food would be much less palatable without good seasoning; however, you wouldn't want to make a meal of salt and pepper alone. There are many elements of a relationship between two people that are more basic, such things as respect, friendship, and common ideals and goals. Dating should be one of the enjoyable means of discovering the kind of person who would be best suited for you in all these vital areas. As you ultimately become more serious in your courtship, you will naturally discover if the one in whom you're interested is warm and considerate.

Also, as you know, there are many times when "showing a little affection" really gets out of hand. Many reputations, as well as lives, are seriously affected when proper restraints are not maintained. All you have to do is look around you in your own school for proof of this.

Maintaining high moral standards is not only important for you but also for society, in spite of what appears to the contrary in some of the trashy books, magazines, and movies that are so prevalent today.

After surveying centuries of mankind's history, the eminent scholars Will and Ariel Durrant wrote: "Sex is a river of fire that must be banked and cooled by a hundred restraints if it is not to consume in chaos both the individual and the group." Unfortunately, some young people whose initial intent is "just to show a little affection" get caught in some of those serious problems that consume and almost destroy them.

It seems to me that it would be most helpful if every young man would recognize his need to become a gentleman, help his date have an exceptionally good time in his company, and help her feel safe in his presence.——*Joe J. Christensen*

Are Latter-day Saint girls exempt from standards of modesty in dress while they are performing in marching or cheerleading groups?

My first reaction to this question is to ask another question: Are we ever exempt from Church standards, whether in dress or behavior? Can we expect the Lord to bend his principles or put them aside for certain occasions? I think the answer has to be no to the general question, but there are some aspects of the specific question about marchers and cheerleaders that we need to examine. For example, does adherence to LDS standards mean a girl in a marching group has to wear a knee-length costume? Perhaps the answer to this question can also be suggested by another question. Should an LDS girl wear a knee-length bathing suit when she goes swimming or a turtleneck gown to a dance? Is a ballerina immodest if she performs in standard ballet attire? Modesty in dress is at least partly dependent upon the appropriateness of a particular costume to the occasion or activity for which it is worn. What is appropriate and modest for one activity may not be for another. We have to exercise judgment and make every effort to obey the spirit of the law.

A shorter-than-knee-length skirt can be appropriate for a marching group or for cheerleaders. But even so, the costume need not be immodest. In fact, a Latter-day Saint girl who is a member of such a group can be a strong voice in the choice of costumes. And she should speak up, insisting that the costume be in good taste, appropriate, and modest. Marchers and cheerleaders are in a very real sense on display. I am sure there is no relationship between the brevity of costume and the excellence of a performance. If her performing group, over her protests, selects an immodest (and hence, inappropriate) costume, a Latter-day Saint girl should most certainly choose in favor of the eternal principle.——*Marilyn Arnold*

*Is it all right for
a Latter-day Saint girl to hitchhike?
When would it not be acceptable?
I hitchhiked recently to my university
during a bus strike.*

If you had lived under the Law of Moses you would have found that indeed there were laws and commandments that covered areas even as specific as this. But as his people have grown more spiritually mature, the Lord has often simply taught them general principles and expected them to make their own decisions according to the light he has given them. As he said, "... it is not meet that I should command in all things." This is just one of many, many areas for which there is no specific revelation handed down as Church doctrine. Nevertheless, the Lord has not left us without guidance in such matters. He has given us leaders to advise us; he has given us parents with more wisdom than we have; and perhaps most important, he has given us the Holy Ghost. You should ask yourself if prior to your recent hitchhiking trip you consulted these sources. You should also ask yourself, seriously, if hitchhiking was absolutely the *only* way for you to get to school. Did you really exhaust all the other possibilities? What did others in your situation do, persons who, like you, had counted on bus transportation?

There can really be no hard and fast rule against asking rides from strangers. Sometimes we have car trouble or find ourselves in other difficult situations that require us to solicit help from others. And there are many good people in the world who are willing to help us when trouble arises. But to me, seeking help under dire circumstances is quite different from purposely starting a journey as a hitchhiking venture, taking up a station on a public highway, thumb extended.

You already know all the sensible reasons for not hitchhiking, especially if you are a girl. In many states hitchhiking is against the law. Certainly the newspapers have convinced us, with grim tales of hitchhikers who became assault or murder victims, that hitchhiking is not safe. And there are reasons that go even beyond these very practical considerations. To hitchhike is to ask for trouble, to invite it. It is to willfully remove ourselves from the care of those who love us and place ourselves completely under the power of those who have no reason to be interested in our welfare. Could you with a clear conscience pray for the Lord's protection on such a venture? It would be like praying to him to keep you warm and then going out in sub-zero weather in only a bathing suit. It would be like trying to address God and Satan at the same time. As Paul said, "Ye cannot drink the cup of the Lord, and the cup of devils: ye cannot be partakers of the Lord's table, and of the table of devils." (1 Corinthians 10:21.)

There is another reason why I think a Latter-day Saint girl should not hitchhike. It makes her look cheap. It tells the world that she really has no moral standards that she cares much about. It suggests that she holds herself cheaply. People, rightly or wrongly, pass judgment on the girl at the side of the road. They assume all kinds of things about her; men expect her to be an "easy mark." This may not be true, but you place yourself at the mercy of such an attitude when you hitchhike.

Even in an emergency it pays to be careful. One time several of my friends and I decided to take a short vacation in the Tetons. We had not realized that with several people and all their luggage in the car, we would not get the gas mileage we had expected. Consequently, we ran out of gasoline in a mountainous area some distance from any town. Our only hope of getting gas before nightfall was to get help from a passing motorist, so we set about to flag down a car. Two men finally stopped for us, local men who seemed harmless enough. Nevertheless, several of us went along to find a service station, because we felt there was safety in numbers. Well, the men were harmless enough, but the bottle of liquor they brought out soon after we were on our way was not. They drank during the whole twenty miles or so that we traveled to find gasoline, and by the time we arrived, they were quite drunk. We could have been in a terrible accident. Going back to our car, we waited and watched at the station until a family came by that was known to the station proprietor, and he asked them if they would give us a ride. Those few extra precautions made our return trip much more pleasant.

If a girl must, under extreme circumstances, ask for a ride from people she does not know, then she should at least take these precautions: (1) Never go alone—and take more than two persons if possible. (2) Accept rides only with families or women, not with men unaccompanied by women or children. (3) Avoid traveling with strangers after dark.——*Marilyn Arnold*

What is the purpose of courtship,
and what is the ideal length
of time a couple should go together
before they get married?

Successful marriage is not a matter of two faultless or perfectly matched people marrying. It is a matter of the mutual adjustment of two people possessing good qualities who are willing to work together for success. This process of working together for success begins during the courtship period.

The courtship period needs definition. Some consider courtship to be the period between engagement and marriage. Others view courtship as a process of involvement, running from the time a couple begin to sense a mutual love for each other on through engagement and marriage. My response deals with the latter definition.

Ideally, courtship is a time when a young couple establish a foundation for a celestial relationship. This involves, of course, working together in worthiness toward temple marriage and all that goes with it. Celestial courtship provides an opportunity for the couple to build a common bond of trust for each other. It is the time to look beyond physical feelings and superficial impressions. There ought be an acquaintance with and acceptance of individual interests, personal habits, families, friends, ambitions, plans for the future, outlook on life, and commitment to important values in life. A couple will want to identify and discuss together their reasons for being in love and also develop that bond of love that goes beyond expression.

Courtship is a time when a couple should learn to communicate openly and freely. If communication is difficult before marriage, it is not likely to improve after marriage. A married couple must be more than man and wife; they must have developed a common bond of friendship. Ideas on everyday activities ought to be shared. Each person needs to learn all he or she can about the other's thoughts and attitudes.

Courtship is a time for a couple to consider other possible questions, such as these: What are their feelings toward children and size of family? Where do they want to live? What occupation will the husband engage in? Will the wife work, and if so, for how long? What are their recreational interests? Do they share a commitment to be totally active in the Church? If so, are they prepared to lend support while meetings are attended and duties accomplished? Will family prayer and family home evening be a regular part of their family life? How well do they handle money? Do they share ideas on how it should be spent? Do they believe in arguing in front of children? How do they handle disagreements that arise? Are both ready to face and accept the responsibilities that marriage will place upon them? How well do they know each other's family? Will there be a good relationship there?

Determining the most desirable length of courtship is similar to determining how long a piece of string should be. Both should be long enough to accomplish the purpose for which they are intended. The courtship period and the engagement period provide a time of transition from single to married status. Therefore, it follows that the courtship should not linger on indefinitely. It is my opinion that couples should not get engaged until they can see far enough ahead to set the approximate date for their wedding. Being engaged with no end in sight often creates difficult problems, and a very short engagement often interferes with the completion of the necessary functions of the courtship.

Length of precourtship acquaintance, one's age, emotional maturity, financial security, and many other factors may affect decisions about the length of courtship. Just bear in mind that time is needed to adequately test a couple's compatibility by checking such matters as those discussed above, to prepare themselves for the acceptance of the responsibilities of marriage, to plan their wedding, and to fully initiate their celestial relationship.——*William Rolfe Kerr*

*How can I know
when I have found
the right person to marry?*

Some say that a person will "know in his heart" when the right person comes along. Others say that if he is wise, he will not "let his heart run away with his head." The basic dilemma of most people in selecting a mate is reflected in the conflicting advice given in these bits of folk wisdom, namely, how much should one rely on feelings and emotions and how much on analysis and reason. Western societies emphasize the importance of the feeling side (you'll know in your heart when you are really in love), whereas when parents choose a mate for their child, as in some Eastern societies, the rational, analytical components are underscored (he comes from a good family; he is intelligent and hardworking; and so forth).

The Latter-day Saint in the mate selection process should be aware of both aspects and try to determine if the decision to marry rests solely on feelings or emotions. If he or she cannot at times coldly and rationally analyze the other person's strengths and weaknesses, then perhaps feelings and emotions are dominating the relationship to the exclusion of reason and analysis. It is possible for reason to dominate in the mate selection process, but this rarely happens in our society.

Just saying that careful thought as well as feelings are important in choosing a mate still leaves unanswered what one should think carefully about. The best answer from both the scriptures and social scientists seems to be, Think carefully about what the two of you have in common. One way to get perspective on this is to climb up the prospective mate's family tree and look around. Many studies show that people who marry within their own group, with similar religious and ethnic backgrounds and socio-economic status, seem to get along better. Do they have the same or similar values? Are they good friends? Do they enjoy the same types of people and activities? Do they agree on issues concerning children? They may not be able to answer yes to all of these questions, but they will at least know which questions raise possible conflicts. This may force them to ask about the risks involved if they were to marry.

By this time you may be asking, "Why all this emphasis on careful thinking and reasoning? Isn't this putting too much emphasis on man's own reasoning powers to the exclusion of God's influence in the lives of people? Can't I just ask God in prayer and then know if this is the right person?"

The scriptures tell us that we should be anxiously engaged in a good cause and do many things of our own free will. (D&C 58:26-29.) Furthermore, we are counseled that it is not good to be commanded in all things. Surely the selection of an eternal companion is a good cause, as well as a very important part of the necessary earth-life experience that we came here to obtain. It obviously requires a good portion of analytical contemplation along with fervent prayer.

The scriptures also counsel that we should not just ask and expect an answer. We are to study a question out in our own minds, attempt to reach a decision, and then diligently seek God's assistance through prayer. (D&C 9:7-9.) If we do not do our part, we can hardly expect God to answer just because we ask. If, however, we do all within our power and then go before

66   the Lord in prayer, he will not abandon us in times of mo-
mentous decision-making, such as in choosing a mate.
Oftentimes the assurance we receive at such times is the
knowledge that God has heard our prayers, accepts our efforts
up to that point, and bids us proceed to the next step.

Many times questions of finding the right person imply that
there is a one and only mate for us, and as soon as that person is
found, eternal bliss will result. This type of thinking tends to
overemphasize the element of discovery and to underestimate
the element of creation. In most instances, acts of creation must
follow the moment of discovery, if that discovery is ever to be
an important one. This seems especially true for selecting an
eternal companion. One can know when he has found the right
person by thinking clearly and searching it out in his own mind,
seeking God's assistance through prayer for a confirmation of
his efforts, and resolving that the finding of a mate is but the beginning of an eternal creation. A person cannot create without
effort. Thus, he may have found the right person now, but without the willingness on the part of both persons to work at it,
they may discover at some time in the future that one or the
other has turned into the wrong person. They should look not
only to the past and present (what kind of person each has been
and is), but also the future (what each is willing to become).
Answers to the latter question may more accurately tell them if
they have found the right person to marry.

If a person has thought carefully about what he and his
prospective mate have in common and has selected a person
who shares many of the same ideals, then there should be few, if
any, real values that need to be compromised. Indeed, one
should receive from his mate the assurance, the well-being, and
the peace of mind necessary to live according to his own values.
Two people who share eternal values and are committed to a
lifetime of effort together should experience few destructive
arguments. They will have disagreements, yes, but as they work
together they should be able to resolve their differences
constructively and increase in that oneness of purpose that leads
unto eternal life.——*Darwin L. Thomas*

What are the requirements
for a person to receive
a temple recommend for marriage?

67

"*The* temple has always been mysterious to me," said Mary, as she and Phil visited with me, her bishop, that Sunday afternoon. They were planning a marriage in the temple in June, and already it was the end of March.

"I have always wondered what goes on inside the temple and can hardly believe that I am old enough to be married there for time and eternity."

"First let me congratulate you for your wisdom in coming to me early and letting me help you with your temple plans," I said. "You know, many young people wait until late in their plans to visit with their bishop, and occasionally this causes real problems. Especially is this true if announcements have already been sent out telling of a planned temple marriage. But most important, let me talk to you about some of the things required of you and Phil to enter the temple and be married there. I congratulate you for your desire to go to this sacred place and there begin your married life together. Those who do so have an eternity of possibilities before them, you know."

Mary asked what the requirements were to enter the temple. "You know, it's really not mysterious," I said, "but rather something that is too sacred to discuss except within the walls of the Lord's holy house. There are several basic requirements for a temple recommend that you and Phil have already accomplished. Let me tell you what they are. You have both been baptized by the authority of the priesthood and have been confirmed members of the Church. Phil, you're already an elder and hold the Melchizedek Priesthood, and that's a requirement. Next, you both need a testimony of the truthfulness of the gospel. President Joseph Fielding Smith said in his book *The Way to Perfection* that no man or woman should ever enter the holy temples of our Father in heaven without having a testimony of the truthfulness of the restored gospel. And you'll each need to have your own endowments before you can be married for time and eternity."

At this point Phil interrupted. "What is having one's own endowment?"

"The endowment," I continued, "is instruction coupled with covenants that prepare us to enter into the highest order of eternal marriage and jointly be candidates for godhood. Brigham Young said of it, 'Let me give you the definition in brief. *Your endowment* is, to receive all those ordinances in the House of the Lord which are necessary for you, after you have departed this life, to enable you to walk back to the presence of the Father, passing the angels who stand as sentinels, being enabled to give them the key words, the signs and tokens, pertaining to the Holy Priesthood, and gain your eternal exaltation in spite of earth and hell.' " (*Journal of Discourses* 2:31.)

"What other requirements are there?" asked Mary.

I then told her how important it was to be personally worthy. "Probably more young couples fail to meet the requirements relating to this than any other," I continued. "There must have been no unrepented moral uncleanliness prior to marriage, including heavy petting, fornication, homosexuality, or similar transgression, because the powers of procreation are most sacred. Only the simplest forms of affection should be expressed between those who date, and when passions become unrestrained during that time, it is most offensive to the Lord. Even immoral thoughts are displeasing to him. If transgressions have occurred, repentance must be complete, including sufficient time lapse before one can be admitted to the temple."

At this point I read to them from the Doctrine and Covenants 97:15-17: "And inasmuch as my people build a house unto me in the name of the Lord, and do not suffer any unclean thing to come into it, that it be not defiled, my glory shall rest upon it; Yea, and my presence shall be there, for I will come into it, and all the pure in heart that shall come into it shall see God. But if it be defiled I will not come into it, and my glory shall not be there; for I will not come into unholy temples."

"Can you see how important it is to be morally clean before entering the Lord's holy place?" I said.

President Marion G. Romney said in the *Improvement Era* (February 1965, p. 120), "God grant that we may be worthy to stand in His presence when we come here. To come unworthily into this temple and receive our endowments will not prove to be a blessing to us."

"I can see that one must be really morally worthy to enter the Lord's house," said Mary.

Then I outlined several other requirements. "One must live the Word of Wisdom, including abstaining from coffee, tea, alcohol, and tobacco. Abusive use of drugs should also be avoided.

And one must live the law of tithing and receive the blessings that come from this expression of unselfishness."

"These things aren't difficult for us," said Phil. "Are there others?"

"Yes," I said. "It's a requirement that you be willing to sustain the local leaders and the General Authorities of the Church. Only as we stand in obedience to the teachings and commandments of the Lord, including those he gives through his living prophet and those who preside with him, can the atonement of Jesus Christ apply to us, and we be worthy to enter the temple. It's important that we be honest in everything we do. We have to be righteous in all that we do, strive to keep all the rules, laws, and commandments of the gospel, and attend sacrament, priesthood, and other meetings designed for our spiritual improvement. And one other thing—you can't have any sympathetic feelings toward any of the apostate groups whose teachings are counter to the accepted doctrines of the Church.

"In summary," I said, "it's required of all who would enter into the temple for the purpose of celestial marriage that they be prepared, worthy, and valiant in the kingdom of God on earth. Then their blessings will abound and the Spirit of the Lord will be felt.

"There is another requirement I'd like to mention," I said. "Because of the sacred nature of celestial or eternal marriage, it becomes doubly important that those who enter into it be prepared to do so. I would almost think that this would require intellectual preparation. Those who would so marry should be mature and in full control of their emotions. They should have, it seems to me, a distinct willingness to share and a commitment to live by principles. Someone getting married in the temple should have the ability to control his life and himself and be willing and able to sacrifice for the future."

Mary and Phil sat thoughtfully for a moment and reflected on our discussion. "Let me read you two sentences from President Harold B. Lee," I said. " 'When you enter a holy temple, you are by that course gaining fellowship with the Saints in God's eternal kingdom, where time is no more. In the temples of your God you are endowed not with a rich legacy of worldly treasure, but with a wealth of eternal riches that are above price. The temple ceremonies are designed by a wise Heavenly Father who has revealed them to us in these last days as a guide and a protection throughout our lives, that you and I might not fail to merit exaltation in the celestial kingdom where God and Christ dwell.' " (*Improvement Era,* June 1967, p. 144.)

"That's quite a list of requirements and lots to ponder," said Mary.

"I agree," I said. "But when you kneel across the altar with your chosen companion and you know you are worthy to be in the house of the Lord, you will personally know that every effort was really worth it."——*Malcolm S. Jeppsen*

What is a temple endowment?
When is it recommended that a Church member
receive the endowment?
Can a twenty-one-year-old girl
who plans to be married in the temple
in the near future receive her endowment
prior to the marriage date?

To comprehend the significance of the temple endowment, it would be well to start with a definition of the *endowment.* The usual dictionary definition of the word *endow* is "to furnish with an income" or "to enrich." Funds, or other properties out of which funds may be made available to educational and eleemosynary organizations and institutions, commonly derived from gratuitous donations or contributions, are referred to as endowments. A person's natural capacity, ability, or power is also referred to as an endowment. Webster defines an endowment in The Church of Jesus Christ of Latter-day Saints as "a course of instruction . . . concerning past and present dispensations and their associated ordinances . . . given in the temples only."

The sum total of all such definitions falls far short of the eternal scope of a temple endowment. The endowment is not limited to a course of instruction concerning past and present dispensations and their associated ordinances. The principles and ordinances of the endowment are timeless; they were established before the world was; they reach into the eternity in both directions and apply more importantly to futurity than to the past, as well as provide guidance, direction, and strength to the present.

The endowment comprehends an enrichment not measured in or by money or other material treasures subject to theft and the corrosion of moth and rust. To receive the temple endowment is to receive the riches of eternity—the knowledge, the power, the keys to unlock the door to the treasures of heaven. To receive the endowment is to receive a course of instruction together with all the keys, powers, and ordinances ordained and revealed by God to prepare his children for eternal life.

The temple endowment was introduced and established in Nauvoo, Illinois, in May 1842, pursuant to an earlier revelation given to the Prophet Joseph Smith, in which the Lord said, in part:

". . . and build a house to my name, for the Most High to dwell therein.

"For there is not a place found on earth that he may come to and restore again that which was lost unto you, or which he hath taken away, even the fulness of the priesthood.

"And verily I say unto you, let this house be built unto my name, that I may reveal mine ordinances therein unto my people;

"For I deign to reveal unto my church things which have been kept hid from before the foundation of the world, things that pertain to the dispensation of the fulness of times.

"And I will show unto my servant Joseph all things pertaining to this house, and the priesthood thereof, and the place whereon it shall be built." (D&C 124:27-28, 40-42.)

Pursuant to his promise, God revealed to Joseph Smith the sacred principles and ordinances of the holy endowment and of eternal marriage into which the endowment leads.

So great and glorious were these principles and ordinances that the Prophet was impressed to share them with a few Saints in a poorly improvised room above a store in Nauvoo, before the Lord's house (the Nauvoo Temple) was completed. He records in his journal, under date of May 4, 1842:

"I spent the day in the upper part of the store . . . (. . . for want of a better place) in council with General James Adams, of Springfield, Patriarch Hyrum Smith, Bishops Newel K. Whitney and George Miller, and President Brigham Young and Elders Heber C. Kimball and Willard Richards, instructing them in the principles and order of the Priesthood, attending to washings, anointings, endowments and the communication of keys pertaining to the Aaronic Priesthood, and so on to the highest order of the Melchizedek Priesthood, setting forth the order pertaining to the Ancient of Days, and all those plans and principles by which any one is enabled to secure the fulness of those blessings which have been prepared for the Church of the First Born, and come up and abide in the presence of the Eloheim in the eternal worlds." (*History of the Church* 5:1-2.)

President Harold B. Lee added another dimension to our understanding of the endowment: "The temple ceremonies are designed by a wise Heavenly Father who has revealed them to us in these last days as a guide and a protection throughout our lives that you and I might not fail of an exaltation in the Celestial kingdom where God and Christ dwell." (*Decisions for Successful Living* [Deseret Book Co., 1973], p. 141.)

Having come to at least some understanding of and appreciation for the temple endowment, the second question logically follows: How soon in life should a person receive this great blessing? The answer is indicated in the journal of the Prophet Joseph Smith, immediately following the account of the revealing of the endowment. He continued in his journal:

"The communications I made to this council were of things spiritual, and to be received only by the spiritual minded: and there was nothing made known to these men but what will be made known to all the Saints of the last days, *so soon as they are prepared to receive,* and a proper place is prepared to communicate them. . . ." (*History of the Church* 5:2. Italics added.)

The answer, then, to the question as to when Church members should receive the endowment cannot be given in terms of age but rather in terms of preparation and readiness to receive. Age, no doubt, is a consideration but not the determining factor. President Joseph F. Smith, for example, received his temple endowment at the age of fifteen years. The Lord was thereby preparing him for a full-time mission to which he was called shortly thereafter. While it is not the current practice to call missionaries at such an early age, our missionaries—male and female—are given their temple endowment prior to their departure to their mission fields in order that they may be endowed with power from on high and given the added strength and guidance so vital to their success.

There is wisdom in the counsel presently being given to young, unmarried members and, more particularly, to young women, that they do not seek the temple endowment until such time as temple marriage is imminent or a full-time mission call has been received. In a *Priesthood Bulletin* of the Church published in February 1973, the following instruction appears: "Church leaders should not urge young, unmarried members to obtain their endowments unless they are to be married in the Temple or are called to serve as missionaries. Members should be authorized to obtain their endowments only when worthiness, age, and maturity justify it."

When we lack worthiness and adequate preparation of mind and heart to receive the blessings of the endowment, it is better that we do not enter into the house of the Lord where the light of truth burns so brightly; for when the light shines upon us, "every man whose spirit receiveth not the light is under condemnation." (D&C 93:32.)

An intriguing question, packed with import, was once asked the Prophet Joseph by the Lord: "What doth it profit a man if a gift is bestowed upon him, and he receive not the gift?" (D&C 88:33.) There is nothing given us in the house of the Lord that does not have its price fixed. We receive the gift by paying the price, and that price is obedience to the law upon which the gift is given; for the Lord has told us that "for all who will have a blessing at my hands shall abide the law which was appointed for that blessing, and the conditions thereof, as were instituted from before the foundation of the world." (D&C 132:5.)

This concept is beautifully expressed by Dr. James E. Talmage:

"The ordinances of the endowment embody certain obligations on the part of the individual, such as covenant and promise to observe the law of strict virtue and chastity, to be charitable, benevolent, tolerant and pure; to devote both talent and material means to the spread of truth and the uplifting of the race; to maintain devotion to the cause of truth; and to seek in every way to contribute to the great preparation that the earth may be made ready to receive her King,—the Lord Jesus Christ. With the taking of each covenant and the assuming of each obligation a promised blessing is pronounced, contingent upon the faithful observance of the conditions." (*The House of the Lord* [Deseret Book, 1974], p. 84.)

Can a man or woman who has an income and who fails to pay an honest tithe enter the temple and, in good faith (meaning a state of mind indicating honesty of purpose and freedom from fraud, deceit, and gross negligence), make covenants of charity and benevolence, and promise to devote (consecrate) his material means to the spread of truth and the building up of the kingdom of God? Parents, bishops, and other church leaders should prepare those who come to the temple to receive the Lord's blessings to do so in good faith.

I recall a conversation I had with a young Northwestern University dental student while I was serving as president of the Chicago Stake. I was interviewing him to hold an office in an elders quorum presidency and learned that he was not a full tithe payer. He assured me that he kept all the other commandments required to hold office but that his income was too small to cover the expenses of going to school and supporting a wife. After counseling him at some length and explaining that if he lacked the faith to pay an honest tithing he lacked the necessary faith to hold the priesthood office or to enter the Lord's house and receive the Lord's blessings, our conference ended. A few days later he called and reported that he was now a full tithe payer. He was soon set apart as a quorum officer. Some time thereafter he and his lovely wife came to my home for a temple recommend. It was a joy to sign those recommends. As they left our home I counseled them to drive their car carefully and observe the traffic laws of the various states through which they must travel, for we needed them in our stake and wanted them to go and return in safety. They assured me they would, and then the young man added with a smile, "I don't think you have to worry about our having an accident in a car we mortgaged to pay our tithing." I love our youth for their faith and devotion.

The third question submitted to me can be answered very briefly. Yes, a young girl who plans a temple marriage in the near future can receive her endowment prior to the date of her marriage, but I would advise her to forgo this privilege until the marriage is imminent and the receiving of the endowment is reasonably near the date set for the temple marriage.

To sum it all up, we in the temple are grateful and happy to see our people—young and old—come to the house of the Lord for their endowments and eternal marriage when, and as soon as, they are worthy and possess the maturity to understand the principles involved, the faith to accept them, and the courage, strength of testimony, and integrity to conform their lives to the covenants that they must make with God.—*John K. Edmunds*

*A*lthough the actual temple marriage ceremony lasts less than five minutes, the beautiful relationship that begins at that altar in God's holy house will extend beyond the grave and throughout eternity, dependent only on the faithfulness of the marriage partners.

Being the crowning ordinance of the gospel of Jesus Christ, this sealing ceremony opens the door to exaltation and eternal lives in the celestial kingdom. Without exchanging those glorious covenants and promises with God and our beloved, we close the door on achieving those celestial goals. The Lord has warned us in no uncertain terms that temple marriage is absolutely essential to our inheriting eternal lives. In the great revelation he gave to Joseph Smith on eternal marriage, the Lord declared: "Verily, verily, I say unto you, except ye abide my law ye cannot attain to this glory." (D&C 132:21.)

In the Salt Lake Temple where I serve as a sealer, the couple to be married may approach marriage in one of two ways. They may go to the temple to receive their endowments and then make an appointment for the marriage ceremony on a subsequent date, or they may proceed directly from the endowment session to the marriage. In any event each couple is given a half-hour reservation of a sealing room where this sacred ordinance will be performed.

The couple is asked to be at the temple an hour before the appointed time so temple officials can check the marriage license and related papers and prepare the necessary documents for the recording of the marriage. The bride then proceeds to the lovely bride's room where she can change into her wedding gown and temple robes. At the same time the bridegroom dresses in his temple clothes. In both cases temple workers are on hand to give very special care and attention to the couple on such an important occasion.

Everything in the temple enhances the sacred importance of the wedding day so that the experience in the house of the Lord is a never-to-be-forgotten event in the lives of both bride and groom.

The sealing room is large enough to seat family and close friends but small enough to provide an intimate atmosphere for all who are present. There could be no more sacred setting for a marriage.

Prior to performing the marriage ceremony the sealer will talk to the couple, giving them solid advice and counsel about their marriage and their new life together. He may point out to them the new dimensions of their lives and give them some guidelines by which they can build a successful relationship in unity and love. He may stress the vital importance of the covenants of an eternal marriage and the responsibility of the couple to live worthy of fulfillment of the celestial blessings that are the promise of a temple marriage. Every sealer draws on his own experience to make these few minutes a very personal prelude to the sealing ordinance. These are very tender moments for the bride, groom, and everyone present.

There are few sights so touching and inspiring as a handsome couple kneeling across from each other at the altar. Often I have asked the groom if he has ever seen anyone more beautiful than his radiant bride. One young man responded, "No artist could paint such a lovely picture." His eloquent reply expresses the feelings of all his fellow grooms on that special occasion.

As the couple gaze into each other's eyes with complete trust and confidence, knowing that they are clean and worthy of exchanging eternal promises with each other and with the Lord, they often shed unrestrained tears of joy during the course of the ceremony. As often as I have repeated the words of that beautiful ceremony, I always sense a real thrill in realizing that I am a conduit between God and the couple in sealing them for eternity. It is the greatest privilege of my life!

Because of the sacred nature of the ceremony, I am unable to share the wording of the marriage. Suffice it to say that the ceremony contains the most glorious promises to which man can aspire. I would encourage you to read Doctrine and Covenants, section 132, to gain understanding of the vital importance of eternal marriage.

I pray with all my heart and soul that you will prepare for a temple marriage. It requires firm faith, personal integrity, prayerful thought, maturity, unselfishness, moral courage—all the virtues that lead to happiness and fulfillment. It requires being a Latter-day Saint in every respect. Nothing is worth the risk of being denied the privilege of a celestial marriage.

From my own experience I can promise you that your preparation for those precious five minutes—and for eternity—is worth it. So live that you may count on such a beautiful beginning to an eternal marriage, confident that your Father in heaven loves you as his children and has prepared the way for you to return to his presence as joint heirs to exaltation and eternal life.——*Robert L. Backman*

*My parents are not active
in the Church and will be unable
to attend my temple wedding.
Since I did not serve a mission
and do not have other relatives
who are members of the Church,
will there be someone in the temple
to help me so I will know
what to do, where to go, etc.?*

Your first experience in the temple is very important. A special effort is made by the temple workers to make it a happy and a spiritual experience so that you will be anxious to return again and again to refresh your memory regarding the covenants you made there and to deepen your knowledge of the endowment given you by your Father in heaven in his holy house.

It is a beautiful thing to have your parents share this experience with you, but when this is not possible, you may come with another relative or a friend who is a worthy temple-recommend holder. If you come alone, the most important thing to keep in mind is that you are actually in the house of the Lord, where there are humble, inspired workers waiting to serve you. The Lord can and will bless you, even though you may be alone.

The minute you enter the temple you are greeted by these workers, and someone is assigned to be with you from then until you leave the temple. If you come with your partner as bride and groom, you will stay together for your interview and the final checking of recommends. After a preliminary, separate ordinance, you are brought together again for the remainder of your stay.

The temple worker accompanying you is aware that this is the first time you have been to the temple and is careful to be understanding, to answer any questions, and to give you step-by-step instructions as the holy ordinances proceed. If a bride has her mother with her, the mother may help her with her wedding dress and be with her to hear the instructions given to the bride. She remains by her daughter's side until the endowment is finished and the bride and groom meet for the wedding.

If you come to the temple alone and wish to have someone with you, a friend may come or one of the patrons attending the session may be asked to accompany you. Often this experience turns into a beautiful and lasting friendship between the patron and the person he or she accompanies through the temple. If you prefer to be alone, the temple workers are always there to give direction and assistance. These provisions are taken to help make you feel at ease and be in the right spiritual frame of mind to understand and appreciate the great blessings given to you that day in the temple.

Parents who are not members of the Church or who are inactive but who wish to be near the temple when you are married are made to feel at home in the comfortable outer foyer of the temple during the time of the endowment and marriage. While there, the matron and a member of the presidency of the temple usually welcome them, visiting with them and answering any questions. When possible, the person who performs the marriage or sealing also visits with the parents. After the marriage, the bride and groom may go to the outer foyer of the temple to join them. Picture taking and friendly greetings are conducted outdoors in front of the temple, with both members and nonmembers of the Church participating. This part of the temple experience frequently plants a desire in the hearts of nonmember or inactive parents to want to know more of what has made their son or daughter so happy in the temple that day.
——*Mary Clarke*

Will I be allowed
to wear my wedding dress
to my temple marriage or sealing?
If so, are there special requirements
that I need to know about before my marriage
so I can design my dress accordingly?

This is your wedding day! From the time you were a little girl you began to weave in your mind dreams of this day—this glorious time when you would have found the perfect man who loved you and wanted you beside him through all the years to come.

You are one of the daughters of Zion—a member of The Church of Jesus Christ of Latter-day Saints. Your marriage this day will have a special quality. You and your sweetheart have kept yourselves clean and pure, and you are one of those blessed couples who are eligible to be married in the house of the Lord—his holy temple. This, you know, will entitle you to receive all the blessings of eternal life if, together, you will be true and faithful.

Years ago you began preparations for this day of days. Recently your mind has been crowded with questions: Can you wear your beautiful wedding-reception dress to your temple ceremony? And your shoes—can they have high heels? Will your mother or someone you love be allowed to assist you in the temple as you dress for your wedding? Can you have outside photographs taken in your wedding dress and veil with the temple in the background? For all these questions you need answers so that your wedding day will be perfect. You want to come to the house of the Lord with assurance and love and joy in your heart, ready to feel his Spirit and receive the blessings reserved for you.

In the Salt Lake Temple, and in all the temples of the Church, the dress requirements are much the same. You can, indeed, wear your lovely bridal gown for your marriage (or temple sealing). It may be made in any appropriate style becoming to you. The gown must be white, including trim. It may be decorated with lace and/or seed pearls or small beads. However, sequin or very showy trim is inappropriate. You may have a train on your gown, but for your convenience, it should be so arranged that you can comfortably carry it. Your wedding gown should have long sleeves and a modestly high neckline. If, for any reason, your gown does not meet the full requirements of the temple, the bride's room has lovely yokes and sleeve linings in materials to match and enhance your gown so that it will be acceptable for your temple ceremony.

The all-white slippers you wear in the temple should have no heels or very low heels and should be simple in style. You may wear a higher heel when you have photographs taken outside in the temple gardens.

Your parents or family members who do not hold temple recommends may wait in the temple foyer while you are being married and then join you in the temple gardens for pictures. In the temple you will not use your "illusion" or wedding veil, but you may bring it with you and use it for your photographs on the temple grounds.

The giving or exchange of wedding rings is not part of the temple marriage ceremony, but it is a beautiful custom and is permitted in the temple. Corsages and wedding bouquets are not used in the temple.

If you desire to use your wedding gown in subsequent temple visits, you will want to design it very simply and probably with removable trim and decoration. Simplicity of dress is in keeping with the spirit in the house of the Lord.

If for some reason you do not have or do not desire to prepare a special wedding gown of your own, you will find lovely wedding dresses in the temple that you can rent for use there.

Your mother or someone close to you may accompany and assist you throughout your temple marriage ceremony (provided, of course, she has her temple recommend).

And now, at last, that most important day of your life is here. As you come to the temple of the Lord, come knowing that the gifts and blessings given you this day will make it possible for you to receive exaltation, eternal life. Yes, come and don your beautiful wedding gown; come with your hair shining and bright; come with your eyes glowing like stars; come to be married in the house of the Lord! But know always that it is your pure heart and clean mind, your love for each other and for all mankind, your faith, your humility, your willingness to walk in his paths and obey his laws that will keep that glorious joy in your hearts.——*Jasmine R. Edmunds*

*What happens when a couple
get a temple divorce?
What happens to the children
in the next life?*

81

As to the first question, we should understand that there is no such thing as a temple divorce. What we refer to as a temple divorce is in fact a cancellation of a temple sealing. When a couple are married in the temple, they not only satisfy the law of the land as to a legal civil marriage, but they are also sealed for time and all eternity in an eternal relationship.

A civil divorce nullifies the marriage so far as the civil law is concerned, but only by a mandate of the president of the Church can the sealing of the couple be cancelled. A cancellation of the sealing is what we are really referring to when we talk about a temple divorce.

When one has been granted a civil divorce after his temple sealing, he must be cleared by the First Presidency before he can be granted a temple recommend by his bishop. After a divorce clearance has been granted by the First Presidency, an application for a cancellation of the temple sealing might be made to the president of the Church. Normally it is the woman who seeks a cancellation of sealing. Since a woman cannot be sealed to two men at the same time, she must have a cancellation of sealing from one before she can be sealed to another.

As to the next question—What happens to the children in the next life?—it is understood that in the case of a cancellation of the sealing of the woman to the man, the sealing of the children to the parents is not cancelled, since the children were born in the covenant, which is a birthright blessing. They remain in the status of the sealing to their parents and can never be sealed to anyone else. The decision as to the parent with whom they will go will be determined by the Lord in the hereafter.

Regarding being born in the covenant, the *General Handbook of Instructions* states, "Children born in the covenant cannot be sealed to anyone, but belong to their natural parents. This rule is not altered by adoption, consent of the natural parents, request of the child after becoming of age or death of the natural parents."

It should be kept in mind that to be born in the covenant is a birthright blessing, and that if in this life a child remains worthy of celestial blessings, regardless of the actions of his parents, he is assured of that birthright and is guaranteed eternal parentage. One's worthiness through living the gospel and keeping the commandments, in this as in all things, is the key to eternal life.——*Elder James A. Cullimore*

Do early marriages tend to end in failure?

*Y*es, yes, yes! It is unusual to find a question that can be answered as simply as this one. Yet I suspect that if you and I were talking together, this answer would not really be very satisfying. You would probably bombard me with a series of follow-up questions, such as: Why are you so sure? Have not some of your friends married quite young and still had successful marriages? What do you mean by early marriage? Since we can't have a dialogue on the topic, let me answer some of the questions that may make the yes-yes-yes answer more understandable.

A friend was married at seventeen, and her husband was a year and a half older. Into that marriage have come eight choice spirits, and by all indications these children will be exceptionally fine young men and women. The two older children have entered college, and the oldest boy will likely enter the mission field by the end of this academic year. The husband-father has been a bishop and is now in a stake presidency. By all criteria I would classify this family as successful, even though the parents were relatively young at marriage. In your own life you can undoubtedly identify examples of successful marriages that started out at a relatively young age. If so, what are we to understand by early marriage?

By early marriage I mean the union between two people who have not had enough experience with life to have become prepared for marriage. Early marriage is marriage between immature people—people who are not spiritually, psychologically, or sociologically grown-up even though they may be physiologically mature. The relationship between chronological age and emotional and social maturity is such that a person in his early to middle twenties will more likely have reached a sufficient level of maturity to be successful at marriage than will a person who is seventeen or eighteen.

A critical sign of immaturity is a failure to know one's own abilities and potentials. This failure to know oneself can be seen in the young child who must receive considerable encouragement before trying something that in fact he can easily do, or in the child who enthusiastically starts piano lessons, loudly announcing his intention to play. He quickly finds that one lesson does not make him a player. He realizes that hours, days, weeks, and years will have to be spent in practice before he can play.

This failure to know oneself, along with a need to have things *now*, plagues early marriages and increases the disaster potential. I recently talked with a high school senior who was engaged to a high school junior, and both felt they must be married as soon as school ended. I asked what he planned to do to earn money for the new family. He didn't have specialized skills but said he had a friend who operated a service station. He was sure he could get a job there. They both wanted the wife to finish high school during their first year of marriage. Further discussion revealed that the girl's parents were deeply upset whenever the topic of marriage came up—which it seldom did in her home.

I came away from that discussion thinking, "Early marriage . . . immaturity . . . they think they must have marriage *now* because it will solve their problems . . . they don't know themselves . . . their experiences do not equip them to meet the demands that society will make on that marriage!"

Early marriages are frequently made by socially immature people. By social maturity I mean having lived long enough to have become an accepted and respected member of important groups in a social space. Considerable research shows that people who are not accepted and respected as children and young adults in their own families have a more difficult time creating strong family ties in their marriage and family life. The religious organization in any society is another important group. Being an accepted and respected member of this group reduces the disaster potential. The third critical group (especially for the husband-father) is that of occupation. The person who is not an accepted or respected member of this strata of society can expect to have a rather high disaster potential in the beginning of marriage. In short, it can be said that a marriage begun too early makes it difficult for that husband and wife to become accepted and respected members of important social groups. When this happens, the disaster potential of early marriage goes up.

It is easy to see why this is true. Few marriages can exist for long in isolation in our contemporary world—even nations find it impossible. Any marriage needs other people outside that marriage to help sustain and nourish it with recognition, encouragement, and help. But most importantly, members of a family need to give order and meaning to their existence. An important dimension of giving meaning to their existence is to create a spot for themselves that, in effect, tells them they are making important contributions not only to themselves but to others. This general feeling of self-worth comes largely from our association with other members of our family, our religious group, or our work worlds. No family is an island.

Realizing that conditions outside the marriage affect what goes on inside leads to another important conclusion. The younger people are at the time of marriage, the more changing they will do as individuals in that marriage. Thus, two young people may be very similar and well suited for each other, but due to the great amount of changing that each will do, they will have a far greater chance of growing apart over the years. The older couple will have made more of their changes and can likely go through life retaining many of their feelings about self and many of the friends they had before marriage. Their basic religious beliefs will probably be retained and strengthened rather than fundamentally changed, and their occupational worlds will likely change little compared to the couple who marry early.

Let me give you some evidence from a study completed not long ago by Professor Kenneth L. Cannon at BYU, which points out many of the things I have been trying to say up to now. This particular study shows what a difference religious commitment makes to the success potential of a marriage. One group in the study consisted of those who, in a sense, did not hold an accepted and respected membership in the religious group (nontemple marriages) while the second group (temple marriages) did. By considering divorce as one indicator of the disaster potential in marriage, important information is contained in the following figures.

Non-Temple Marriages

Number of couples in each group	45	100	62
Bride's age at marriage	17 or younger	18-19	20 or older
Percent in each age group divorced after 13 years of marriage	33	8	6

Temple Marriages

Number of couples in each group	25	96	91
Bride's age at marriage	17 or younger	18-19	20 or older
Percent in each age group divorced after 13 years of marriage	4	3	3

The nontemple marriages and the temple marriages were from similar social and educational levels. The findings of this study are consistent with what has been said in this answer up to now, namely, being an accepted and respected member of a religious group reduces the disaster potential of early marriages. Note that only 4 percent of those with temple marriages were divorced within 13 years compared to 33 percent of the nontemple marriages where the bride's age was 17 or younger.

I'm reminded of the scriptural injunction that a person shall leave his father and mother and cleave unto his mate, and they shall become one—not for a day or year, but for an eternal lifetime. Each person in the process of making the decision to leave father and mother must ask: Have I lived long enough and have I experienced enough of life to know my own abilities and potentials? Am I mature enough to know that much of what I want now can best be acquired by work and sacrifice today for a more meaningful tomorrow? Do I leave my mother and father with their blessing because I have earned their love and respect? Has my life to this point earned the acceptance, respect, and admiration of the Church in the persons of the bishop and the stake president? When I look at myself, do I honestly feel, "I am what I am, no more and no less. But I find it good because my father, the father of my ward, and my Father in heaven find me good."

If these questions can be answered not with a boisterous and hollow yes, but with a deep, quiet affirmation coming from success with life and people, then the blessings of eternal lives shall flow unto you. Your decision to leave father and mother will not be an invitation to disaster but rather a promise of returning to the Father of all with those you love most.——*Darwin L. Thomas*

Should a girl worry about not getting married?

No. Worry does not solve a problem nor is it even an enjoyable activity.

It is normal for a Latter-day Saint girl, who knows that marriage and motherhood are ordained of God and that the family unit may continue throughout eternity, to look hopefully toward a happy marriage in this life. She should continue to do this. She should, however, keep in mind that marriage age patterns differ widely from country to country and culture to culture, even from family to family. Thus, no specific chronological age for marriage could be given that would have universal application.

In American culture, for example, there are unnumbered individuals who marry in their late teens yet mature into wise and happy marriage partners. Conversely, numerous late-in-life marriages are exceptionally happy and will be eternally rewarding.

The marriage ceremony itself does not guarantee happiness and personal fulfillment. Divorce court records confirm this statement.

Every girl should be continuously engaged in constructive activities that will prepare her to be a happy and valuable person. This will be the result of living in harmony with gospel teachings and ideals. If possible, she should acquire specific vocational training, including homemaking skills. Where possible, she should engage in activities that give her opportunities to make new friends and to meet eligible and desirable men.

She should learn that the truly happy woman is one who considers life an enriching experience and who knows the joy of unselfish service to others. She should not be unduly concerned about her age, but very much concerned about the quality of her personal life.

She should also be aware that the Lord will bless her if she continues to keep the commandments and be worthy. President Harold B. Lee wrote:

"You young women advancing in years who have not yet accepted a proposal of marriage, if you make yourselves worthy and ready to go to the house of the Lord and have faith in this sacred principle, even though the privilege of marriage does not come to you now, the Lord will reward you in due time and no blessing will be denied you. You are not under obligation to accept a proposal from someone unworthy of you for fear you will fail of your blessings." (*Decisions for Successful Living* [Deseret Book, 1973], p. 129.) —— *Alberta H. Christensen*

How do women share the priesthood?
How does it apply to an unmarried woman?

President Joseph Fielding Smith said that the priesthood is the power and authority of God delegated to man to act in all things for the salvation of men. It is for the benefit of all members of the Church, men and women, children and youth, married and single.

Latter-day Saint women have always shared in its glorious blessings and privileges. The following are some of the more apparent ways in which I have shared in the blessings of the priesthood in my parental home, with my husband, and now that my husband is no longer living.

1. My ancestors were taught the gospel through the power and authority of the priesthood, and that made it possible for me to have the life in the Church I now live.

2. I received a name and a father's blessing to identify and bless me throughout my life.

3. I was baptized for the remission of my sins, and thus the door to my Heavenly Father's kingdom was opened to me.

4. I was confirmed and received the gift of the Holy Ghost, through which I can discern truth from error and be guided throughout my life.

5. Through the sacrament administered by priesthood bearers, I have the privilege of renewing my covenants with my Father in heaven and having his Spirit with me.

6. At the hands of priesthood authority, I received a patriarchal blessing, which, predicated on my faithfulness, gives me special knowledge as well as direction and comfort.

7. I have received counsel and advice from inspired priesthood bearers, such as my bishop and my home teachers.

8. I have been blessed and comforted and even healed when I have been sick and sorrowing and suffering.

9. Through priesthood power, I can have my sins remitted with the sanction and blessing of God.

10. I have been called to serve God by priesthood authority, and my soul has been greatly enlarged by such opportunities.

11. I have witnessed the thwarting and dispelling of evil forces by priesthood power, and this gives me a reassuring peace and security.

12. My home is blessed by home teachers who give me special service as I live alone.

This is only a partial list of the many ways in which I have shared in priesthood blessings. All of these privileges and more can come equally to men and women, married or single. Marriage is not necessarily the only medium through which women share the priesthood. Celestial marriage and the establishment of eternal homes and families are, of course, the highest blessings of the priesthood on this earth, but marriage alone does not insure such blessings.

Women who are married to bearers of the Melchizedek Priesthood can and must look to their husbands to bless them and perform the necessary priesthood ordinances for them. Single women and those whose husbands do not have the authority to perform priesthood functions have the right to request such blessings from brethren who have authority—their fathers and brothers, their home teachers, and their priesthood leaders.

Priesthood bearers are under solemn obligation to respond to such requests. What a responsibility for men to bear—to be worthy at any time to receive inspiration, for the "rights of the priesthood are inseparably connected with the powers of heaven, and . . . the powers of heaven cannot be controlled nor handled only upon the principles of righteousness." (D&C 121:36.)

Every girl who looks forward to the time when all things will be perfected should prepare herself, taking advantage of and being blessed by the sacred and holy priesthood functions.—— *Hortense H. Child*

What kinds of activities are acceptable on the Sabbath?

*P*erhaps every concerned person has asked that question, if only of himself. And well he might, for no commandment has been spelled out more specifically, emphasized more consistently, or been ignored more generally: "Remember the sabbath day, to keep it holy. Six days shalt thou labour, and do all thy work: But the seventh day is the sabbath of the Lord thy God: . . . For in six days the Lord made heaven and earth, the sea, and all that in them is, and rested the seventh day: wherefore the Lord blessed the sabbath day, and hallowed it." (Exodus 20:8-11.)

Among those who want to obey the Lord's commandments, there is wide and honest divergence of thought. Such divergence is understandable. There are legitimate areas for interpretation, but we need to interpret in the light of scripture. You can rationalize, justify, or quibble with your conscience, or you can listen to the Lord:

"If thou turn away . . . from doing thy pleasure on my holy day; and call the sabbath a delight, the holy of the Lord, honourable; and shalt honour him, not doing thine own ways, nor finding thine own pleasure, nor speaking thine own words:

"Then shalt thou delight thyself in the Lord; and I will cause thee to ride upon the high places of the earth, and feed thee with the heritage of Jacob thy father: for the mouth of the Lord hath spoken it." (Isaiah 58:13-14.)

The import of this and other scriptures is that the purpose of the Sabbath is to nourish the spirit. What nourishes my spirit may not sustain yours, but if we both have an eye clearly on the purpose of the Sabbath, a mobile measuring rod is adequate and relatively accurate. Does the admonition "not doing thine own ways, nor finding thine own pleasure" suggest anything about golf, skiing, movies, baseball, and like pursuits? It does to me.

Writing to her son John, Susannah Wesley said, "Would you judge the lawfulness or unlawfulness of pleasure, then use this rule: Whatever weakens your reason, impairs the tenderness of your conscience, obscures your sense of God, takes off your relish of spiritual things, increases the authority of your body over your mind; *that* then to you is sin."

Using this standard, each person may decide for himself what may best be done on the Lord's day. This puts the burden where the Lord intended—on the shoulders of the individual. Apply this rule to the many activities of your Sabbath day, for spiritual decay may result in you as surely from your carelessness as from willful design. The higher joys of life require self-discipline and training.

Activities that would impede spiritual growth in my thirteen-year-old were not a problem when he was younger. Added maturity requires a finer interpretation.

We have been directed to study and to learn, but wouldn't the best learning for the Sabbath be about things spiritual? Some college students maintain that they get better grades when they study six days of the week and use Sunday to be refreshed. This is not happenstance—it is the Lord's way. Try it! ". . . the Lord made heaven and earth, and on the seventh day he rested, and was refreshed." (Exodus 31:17.)

In this temporal world we must be concerned daily with material needs and wants. An all-wise Father, anticipating this, set aside a special day lest many of us not take the time to nourish the spiritual part of us—that which ultimately matters most. William E. Berrett has said, "God is not waiting to whip us or to punish us for breaking the Sabbath day. What we are will be reward or punishment enough."

This, then, is the heart of the matter. The Sabbath was made for our good—not to enslave the spirit, but to feed it. And when the spirit is fed, the Sabbath day becomes the remarkable blessing that the Lord intended it to be.

The Lord has said, "Ye shall keep my sabbaths, and reverence my sanctuary: . . . And I will . . . establish my covenant with you . . . and I will walk among you, and will be your God, and ye shall be my people." (Leviticus 26:2, 6, 9, 12.)
——*Russell C. Harris*

Should I pay tithing
on money my parents give me
if they have already paid tithing
on that money?

Because of the many questions about tithing that are received by the General Authorities, the First President addressed a letter on March 19, 1970, to presidents of stakes and missions, bishops of wards, and presidents of branches. They referred to Doctrine and Covenants 119:3-4, which reads: "And this shall be the beginning of the tithing of my people. . . . those who have been thus tithed shall pay one-tenth of all their interest annually; and this shall be a standing law unto them forever, for my holy priesthood, saith the Lord."

After quoting this scripture, the First Presidency said: "No one is justified in making any other statement than this. We feel that every member of the Church should be entitled to make his own decision as to what he thinks he owes the Lord, and to make payment accordingly." They did, however, point out that "interest" is understood to mean "income."

At the close of each year every member of the Church is invited to attend tithing settlement with his or her bishop (or branch president), at which time the bishop should be told whether or not the member is a full tithe payer.

Young people should make it a matter of prayer and should consult with their parents if they have any question as to what they should consider income and in deciding how much tithing to pay. They may also seek counsel from their bishop.

The Lord has promised great blessings to those who pay tithes and offerings. We read in Malachi 3:8-10: "Will a man rob God? Yet ye have robbed me. But ye say, wherein have we robbed thee? In tithes and offerings? . . . Bring ye all the tithes into the storehouse, . . . and prove me now herewith, saith the Lord of hosts, if I will not open you the windows of heaven, and pour you out a blessing, that there shall not be room enough to receive it."

The payment of tithing is a private matter between the individual member and the Lord, with the bishop, as the Lord's servant, receiving an accounting for the contribution.

When you have been completely honest with the Lord, a feeling of peace will enter your heart, and you will have no doubt that you are a full tithe payer. Keep in mind the Lord's direction to pay tithes on all your interest (or income); counsel with your parents; consider the blessings promised to those who pay their tithes and offerings; and then make your own decision. As you strive to live this commandment and all of the other commandments of the Lord, you may expect his Spirit to be with you to strengthen and guide you in other decisions of your life.——*Bishop Victor L. Brown*

*Why is fasting so important
and how can we make it work?*

Many of us "repent" of the same sins again and again, but we don't repent of sinning. For instance, we may be lazy or selfish or cowardly or prideful or bad tempered or impure or irreverent or whatever, and from time to time temporarily feel sorry and repentant over the unhappy consequences that follow, but these habits and tendencies may still persist. Unless we change our life-style by rooting out of our nature these deeply imbedded habits and dispositions, we will continue on in a self-deceiving, circular process of making and breaking resolutions to change and improve.

We simply can't repent of our sins unless we repent of our sinning, unless we change our life-style and our basic habit patterns. In other words, we need to change our method of changing ourselves. We need a power source to help us, one that is stronger and more penetrating than the strength and depth of these habits.

The gospel is that power source, and fasting is one gospel practice that, I believe and have discovered for myself, helps immeasurably to open up and release those divine powers on our nature.

Why so, you ask?

I believe this happens in three ways. First, voluntarily going without food and water is physical, concrete. It represents a break in eating itself. We take charge of our own appetites, which in my opinion is a first step in mastering our passions and in placing our own spirit under the direct influence of the Holy Spirit. After forty days of fasting, Christ's own first temptation was to his appetites—then to his passions (pride, vanity) and ultimate desires and motives. The body is a good servant but a bad master.

Second, fasting humbles and subdues our spirit. We become aware of our limitations and our dependency on our Creator and his creations (food) for life itself. As the Holy Spirit works on us, we become more sensitive to the unseen realities; our awareness of our shortcomings and true spiritual nature enlarges; our sense of need for a Savior and faith in Christ as our Savior increases; and our desire and ability to fully confess and repent deepens.

Third, these spiritual endeavors will focus and unify our thinking and feeling so we can renew our covenant relationship with the Lord. When our minds are truly made up, we keep the promises we make. The sacrament is the ordained, divine channel to express these promises and commitments—to renew our covenants. We witness or promise to take upon ourselves his name and keep his commandments, which would include both his general commandments given through his prophets, ancient and modern, and his personal commandments given through his Holy Spirit to our conscience.

As we promise or covenant, the Lord covenants. He promises us his Spirit, which is the key to every good thing in time and in eternity. Such a releasing of the powers of godliness into our lives through faith in Christ, repentance through his power, and covenant making with him will enable us to overcome deeply imbedded habits and dispositions and to gradually become a partaker of the divine nature.

94

I believe that just as the Lord told his disciples that certain spiritual blessings can only come by a faith born of both prayer and fasting (see Matthew 17:14-21), so also certain malignant sinful dispositions and cancerous habit patterns can only be broken by a faith and faithfulness inspired by both prayer and fasting.

Just as we can be, in one sense, active in the Church without being active in the gospel, so also can we fast and not receive the above-mentioned benefits. I offer four suggestions regarding how to fast:

1. *Divine purpose and spirit.* Prepare to fast. Pray for the true spirit of fasting. Think about your spiritual needs and/or about others' physical and spiritual needs. Fast in order to come unto the Lord, to be more like him. Fast from worldliness as well as food, from anything that causes static in your spirit.

2. *Prayer.* This means two-way communication. Listen as well as express. Be very open and receptive to the still, small voice. Don't counsel the Lord on how to bless you; rather, express a desire to take counsel from him.

3. *Feast.* Savor (treasure, meditate on, adore, and worship) his love and his word. Prayerfully ponder the scriptures when you otherwise would be eating, or at other appropriate times.

4. *Serve.* In various ways get outside yourself in love. (Study Isaiah 58.) Give of yourself. Pay your fast offerings, the cost of two missed meals, to the poor through the priesthood. Bear testimony at fast and testimony meeting. Express love and appreciation to your loved ones, leaders, and teachers. Forgive. Make reconciliation with any who are offended or who offend.

Remember, getting bogged down in a lot of introspective self-analysis will serve to undermine the spirit of resolute and devoted service.

Two cautions:

1. *Avoid extremism in fasting.* Sometimes it's easier to try to work on our relationship with God through fasting, prayer, and scripture study than to love and serve his other children or to repair broken human relations. Just as we can sometimes avoid confronting our real spiritual need to change and repent by intellectualizing about gospel principles, so also can we escape dealing with pulsating spiritual needs and service hungers by theatrical and/or excessive fasting. Unless otherwise directed by the Spirit to fast more frequently, we can gain the blessings of fasting by following the Church practice of fasting for two

consecutive meals once a month on the designated fast Sunday.

✗ 2. *Don't take fasting lightly.* Fasting and prayer can literally release the powers of heaven in our lives. We shouldn't toy and play games with these principles or they will turn to our condemnation, and then we will harden to them.

When we really want to change or to undertake any worthy project requiring fasting and prayer for God's help, we had better be prepared for things to happen according to our needs and his will in his time rather than for our wants and our will in our time. We may be given very difficult and trying experiences, but if we stay true and faithful, all things will work together for our good; and we will come to a divine perspective and see how the Lord was fashioning us to his service and was making us "fishers of men."

Finally, let us remember that any time we break our addiction to anything, whether it be drugs, certain foods, or habits, we will go through a certain painful withdrawal process. For instance, when we fast, we may experience headaches caused by withdrawing from certain foods to which we have become addicted. We then may become edgy and irritable and lose the whole spirit of the fast. But if we are aware of the forces at play and stick with it, we can experience a degree of physical cleansing and breaking of the food addiction in addition to conquering a naturally bad temper.

These physical illustrations have many spiritual parallels, in my opinion. Never abort second birth processes because of the labor pains.——*Stephen R. Covey*

*Is it against Church standards
to drink cola beverages
or any other beverage
containing caffeine?*

The Word of Wisdom is a guide to strengthening the body and mind and keeping them healthy so the spirit of the individual can function without impairment. If we understand the Word of Wisdom properly, we will do all things necessary to avoid weakening the marvelous temples the Lord has given us to house our spirits.

The 89th section of the Doctrine and Covenants says: "And again, verily I say unto you, all wholesome herbs God hath ordained for the constitution, nature, and use of man." (V. 10.) We should take note of the word *wholesome* and always consider whether or not the things we take into our bodies are wholesome.

The scripture continues, "All these to be used with prudence and thanksgiving." (V. 11.) Consider the word *prudence.* Would eating a whole apple pie or a cake or watermelon at one sitting be prudent? It is contrary to the principles embodied in the Word of Wisdom concerning taking an excess of anything into our bodies.

Two tests we can employ, then, as we question the use of any food or beverage are: Is it wholesome? Is it prudent?

As we all know, some of us need more rest than others. This same principle implies that we should not tax our bodies beyond good judgment. Finally, remember that the Lord has counseled: "For behold, it is not meet that I should command in all things; for he that is compelled in all things, the same is a slothful and not a wise servant; wherefore he receiveth no reward." (D&C 58:26.)

We know that cola drinks contain the drug caffeine. We know that caffeine is not wholesome or prudent for use in our bodies. It is only sound judgment, therefore, to conclude that cola drinks and any others that contain caffeine or other harmful ingredients should not be used.

"And all saints who remember to keep and do these sayings, walking in obedience to the commandments, shall receive health in their navel and marrow to their bones;

"And shall find wisdom and great treasures of knowledge, even hidden treasures;

"And shall run and not be weary, and shall walk and not faint.

"And I, the Lord, give unto them a promise, that the destroying angel shall pass by them, as the children of Israel, and not slay them. Amen." (D&C 89:18-21.) —— *Bishop H. Burke Peterson*

My nonmember friends seem to know
a lot about the Church's
financial system and business interests.
They say we own controlling interests
in many national companies,
some of which manufacture products
that are against our standards,
such as liquor and tobacco.
What should I tell them?

Briefly you could quote the Church's general policy to your friends: We do not own nor do we seek controlling interest in any major national company. In addition, the Church does not buy securities in any corporation that manufactures such products as cola drinks or alcoholic beverages, publishing companies that print materials not consistent with our standards, or tobacco companies.

At times people donate to the Church properties or securities that would not be consistent with the above principles, but these are sold on the open market soon after they are received.

The Church still owns a few industries that were started out of necessity during pioneer times. They helped to establish the economy, and they are still functioning. These pioneer industries include such companies as the Beneficial Life Insurance Company. We also own support industries such as the Beehive Clothing Mills, *Deseret News,* and Deseret Press, which help in the day-to-day work of the Church. However, many of the original pioneer companies, such as Zion's Bank and ZCMI, are no longer owned by the Church.

The Church does own some agricultural property. In times of need this could easily be converted to welfare production. Of course, all welfare farms are locally owned and operated by the various wards and stakes. The welfare program yields a great variety of produce, which, with the fast offerings, is used for the welfare of those in need.

The financial foundation of the Church is its faithful, devoted membership. The great bulk of our income comes from the tithes and offerings of these faithful members. This income is budgeted according to established directions set down by the Lord in section 120 of the Doctrine and Covenants: "Verily, thus saith the Lord, the time is now come, that it [tithing] shall be disposed of by a council, composed of the First Presidency of my Church, and of the bishop and his council, and by my high council; and by mine own voice unto them, saith the Lord."

The council of the disposition of tithes today is composed of the First Presidency, the Council of the Twelve, and the Presiding Bishopric.

The greatest portion of Church expenditures goes toward meetinghouse construction and maintenance and to the education system, which includes seminaries and institutes, Church schools in underdeveloped countries, Brigham Young University, and Ricks College. The remainder is spent on other activities, including missionary and temple work, internal communications and administrations of the Church, and the printing, translation, and distribution of manuals and teaching materials.

All of the funds of the Church are considered sacred and dedicated to furthering our Father's work on the earth, and they are managed prayerfully and with inspiration.——*President N. Eldon Tanner*

Should college students and other single persons get involved in food storage programs?

Food storage is not only a protection against emergencies; it is also a sound principle from an economic and time management point of view. Regularly used foods (as well as other essentials, such as toilet articles and notebook paper) bought in quantity can mean savings to the purchaser not only in money, but also in time.

If food storage is used in day-to-day living, not just stored away to keep one alive in an extreme emergency, it is a sound principle for students and single people as well as families. Obviously, amount of storage space and permanency of residency would have to be qualifying factors.

As with all counsel from Church leaders, this advice to keep a reserve supply of food and other essentials on hand brings joy to him who obeys it by providing security, better money management, and increased convenience. The counsel is not just for survival; it is also for a more practical and satisfying day-to-day life-style.——*Winnifred Jardine*

Should a nonmember take the sacrament when attending church with a member?

One of the best opportunities for acquainting nonmembers with the spirit and teachings of the gospel is in our church meetings. As part of the nonmember friendshiping responsibility each of us has, we should invite our friends and acquaintances to go with us to Sunday School and sacrament meeting as well as the appropriate auxiliary meetings. However, if the sacrament is to be passed, we should explain to the nonmember in advance that the sacrament is for members to renew the covenant of baptism that they made when they joined the Church. Since the nonmember has not yet been baptized, there is no need for him to take the sacrament. One could explain also that quite often we have nonmembers in our meetings, and, of course, they don't take the sacrament either, so it is neither unusual nor embarrassing for someone not to take the sacrament.

"And again I say unto you, ye shall not cast any out of your sacrament meetings who are earnestly seeking the kingdom—I speak this concerning those who are not of the church." (D&C 46:5.)——*Elder Loren C. Dunn*

*W*e should not use playing cards because the prophets of God
have counseled against it. That in itself should be sufficient
reason to leave them alone. There are, however, other reasons we
could consider. The greatest loss of power that we have in this
world is the loss that results from the failure of individuals to
reach their potential. There are many reasons for this, but
perhaps one of the most important is failure to use time effectively.

Life is short at best. Furthermore, no matter who we are, we
pass through life but once, and whatever record we make is
made forever. Unless we put purpose into our living, the hours
can slip by and get away from us without our having very much
to show for them. Let us think for a moment or two about the
letters of the alphabet. There are only twenty-six of them in the
English alphabet. We may repeat them all frontwards and
backwards, but they have no meaning when so used because
they have not been put together with purpose or direction. The
result is quite different when they are creatively put together,
however, and the end product may be great poetry, prose, songs,
hymns, scientific papers, and so forth.

Ernest Hemingway once said that he found it necessary to
rewrite the opening chapters of his books up to fifty times
before he felt they were ready for public consumption. By working at it in this way he wrote "easy reading."

Robert Ripley, the "Believe It or Not" man, once pointed
out that "a plain unfinished bar of iron is worth five dollars.
This same bar of iron when made into horseshoes is worth
$10.50. If made into needles it is worth $355. If made into pen-
knife blades it is worth $3,285, and if turned into balance
springs for watches, that identical bar of iron becomes worth
$250,000." (Gore Michael, "How to Organize Your Time," *Per-
sonal Success Program* [Garden City, New York: Nelson Double-
day, 1959], p. 3.)

As it is with this bar of iron, so it is with time. Many people
are able to make horseshoes out of each golden hour of time,
but very few have the ability to make of it balance springs for
watches.

Let us keep these things in mind as we think about playing
cards. Such an activity can take up a lot of time. When we use

our time that way, are we using it effectively? There is some fellowshiping in association with others, to be sure, but aren't there better ways for us to use our limited time?

Let us not overlook the fact that some of life's greatest accomplishments have been made by persons who have used their so-called spare time to develop special talents that they possessed. Einstein was a student of mathematics, trained to be a university teacher; but when he could not land a teaching appointment, he took a job as a routine examiner of patent applications in the patent office of Bern, Switzerland. This allowed him ample leisure time, which he devoted to his special talent for mathematics. In 1905 he startled the academic world with the most influential thesis since Newton's laws of gravity, his special theory of relativity. Buttressed by three other papers that he published at the same time, he reshaped the world's fundamental approach to physics and fathered the intellectual revolution that has made possible the achievements of nuclear science. He let his talent be his guide.

Alexander Graham Bell began as a teacher of teachers of the deaf and thus became interested in the mechanics of speech. When he became a professor of physiology at Boston University, he pursued the study of electrical transmission of sound in his spare time and invented the telephone. He had an original idea and devoted his free time to perfecting it.

John S. Bonnell once wrote, "Why do so many people fail to catch hold of the abundant and happy life?" He stated that there are three reasons: (1) They lack purpose. As Voltaire put it, they are like an oven that is always heating but never cooking anything. (2) They lack staying power. At the first taste of success they begin to slow down, to turn aside, or to falter. (3) They make no genuine effort to correct their faults. ("Putting Purpose into Your Life," Pageant, January 1963, p. 100.)

We all have the same amount of time at our disposal each day we live—twenty-four hours. How are we going to use it? We make that choice because we have our free agency. Let us not squander or waste our days away, for if we do, we will end up with many blanks in our lives where there could have been a rich harvest of worthwhile, satisfying living.——*Elder William H. Bennett*

Is there any reason
       or Church doctrine that would suggest
       that I should not have
       my ears pierced?

_____

When I was in a jeweler's shop the other day, I asked the jeweler, "Are girls having their ears pierced now?" He answered, "They are really going for it now," and he brought out a velvet-lined tray full of earrings for pierced ears.

Piercing the earlobes in order to insert earrings is a vogue that comes and goes. It was the only means in biblical times, it would seem, for women to wear earrings. Gold earrings were recognized not only as ornaments but also as items of value. Perhaps one of the earlier mentions of earrings being used is in the Bible when the servant of Jacob, seeking a kinswoman as a wife for Isaac, presented Rebekah with bracelets and gold earrings. The King James account reads, ". . . and I put the earring upon her face, and the bracelets upon her hands." (Genesis 24:47.)

When this was studied in a Sunday School class, a Lebanese sister said, "I suppose that would be a nose ring"—which did not appeal to my taste. It is interesting to find that the account in the Inspired Version of the Bible reads, "And I gave the earrings unto her, to put into her ears, and the bracelets upon her hands." (Genesis 24:51.) This would indicate that the earrings of Rebekah were to go *into* her ears.

In some instances the Old Testament tells of the Israelites collecting their gold earrings to melt them down for the golden calf (Exodus 32:2-4) and to contribute to the adornment of the tabernacle (Exodus 35:22).

Today there are other means of fastening earrings to the ear, so there is not the necessity of piercing the earlobes. The only credible reason I have heard given for piercing ears is where the earrings are of great value, such as diamond earrings, and the wearer wishes to avoid losing them.

I do recall as a young girl how ugly pierced earlobes looked to me. A relative who was born in the 1870s had had her ears pierced as a teenage girl. It was very popular at that time in Salt Lake City. However, this woman did not always wear earrings, and the perforations were most ugly to me.

The craze to pierce or not to pierce seems to occur and recur. I know of no pronouncement or stand that Church authorities have made in this regard. I recall with what disfavor I looked upon one of my granddaughters piercing her ears. I believe she did pierce them but then let them grow together again.

There are some people to whom the practice is repugnant and others who feel comfortable with it, so I would think the decision would be an individual one that each girl and her parents should reach together.——*Marianne C. Sharp*

*What do you think about
the use of hypnotism?*

Historically, the leaders of the Church have spoken against the Saints' using or experimenting with hypnotism, as well as participating in mind-control courses. In 1902 John W. Taylor of the Council of the Twelve said, "I want to lift up my voice and say, that it is an abomination in the sight of the Lord our God." (*Conference Report,* April 1902, p. 76.)

Francis M. Lyman of the Council of the Twelve said, "From what I understand and have seen, I should advise you not to practice hypnotism. For my own part I could never consent to being hypnotised or allowing one of my children to be. The free agency that the Lord has given us is the choicest gift we have. As soon, however, as we permit another mind to control us, as that mind controls its own body and functions, we have completely surrendered our free agency to another; and so long as we are in the hypnotic spell—and that is as long as the hypnotist desires us to be—we give no consent in any sense whatever to anything we do. The hypnotist might influence us to do good things, but we could receive no benefit from that, even if we remembered it after coming out of the spell, for it was not done voluntarily. The hypnotist might also influence us to do absurd and even shocking, wicked things, for his will compels us.

"Hypnotism is very much like the plan that Satan desired the Father to accept before this earth was peopled. He would make them do good and save them in spite of themselves. The Savior, on the other hand, proposed to give free agency to all, and save those who would accept salvation. Our Father rejected Satan's plan, and sacrificed a third part of his children for the sake of upholding this true principle, that men shall have the right to act for themselves, and shall be responsible for their own actions." ("Shall We Practice Hypnotism?" *Improvement Era* 6 [April 1903]: 420.)

An item in the *Priesthood Bulletin* of August 1972 says: "Reports have been received of unfortunate results to persons engaging in group hypnosis demonstrations or in popular mind control courses of study. There are reports that some Church leaders have arranged hypnosis demonstrations as a means of entertainment. Leaders should advise members of the Church against participating in such activities. Certainly, they should not be sponsored or encouraged by leaders of the Church as has been reported."

I have seen hypnotism used with varied results; and having seen it used, I am convinced that when a person submits to hypnotism, he surrenders part or all of his will to another person. In a real sense he loses his free agency for the period of time he is hypnotized and perhaps for periods of time in the future should he be given a posthypnotic suggestion at the time of his hypnosis. No one really realizes how powerful an influence or how unusual a phenomenon a hypnotic trance is, and contrary to many current expressions by hypnotists, people can be made to do things under hypnosis that normally, morally, they would not do. Furthermore, it is difficult to realize how great the temptations are to a therapist when he has total control of another human being.

It is even difficult to decide whom to have care for your body. Some people with apparently good credentials may not be the best surgeons or physicians when judged by their peers, and yet, each of us must choose someone to care for his physical person on the basis of the best criteria he has and as carefully as he can. If his choice is poor, perhaps the worst that can happen is that his body may not be as healthy or heal as fast as it might have if he had made a better choice.

But to whom do you trust your immortal soul? How can you adequately choose someone to whom you can freely give your free agency? your moral will? To what person do you surrender your moral will for the use of his entertainment, or for the entertainment of others, or for the purpose of supposedly helping you with your problems—for example, losing weight, rejecting bad habits, or recalling childhood problems? Who is that trustworthy? This is the basis and the real crux of the problem. Who is so trustworthy as to be allowed to tamper with the eternal soul? At the present time, as a direct answer to the question, "What do you think about the use of hypnotism?" it is my belief that hypnosis is not to be actively engaged in by members of the Church.——*Homer Ellsworth*

*Are there ever any circumstances
that justify not accepting
a Church position?*

In the Church we do not aspire to nor seek positions. Rather, we are called through inspiration by those in authority. It is not uncommon for the one receiving the call to consider himself inadequate for the assignment. He, of course, is inadequate if left to his own abilities. It is essential that each worker in the Church enjoy the companionship of the Spirit of the Lord if he is to be effective in carrying out his responsibilities.

In considering our answer to the priesthood officer extending the call, we should remember Nephi's response to his father Lehi when he was asked to return to Jerusalem with his rebellious brothers to obtain the plates of brass. Notwithstanding the apparent impossible nature of the assignment, Nephi displayed his faith in the Lord when he said, "I will go and do the things which the Lord hath commanded, for I know that the Lord giveth no commandments unto the children of men, save he shall prepare a way for them that they may accomplish the thing which he commandeth them." (1 Nephi 3:7.)

I witnessed this same kind of faith a few years ago in New York City. I was there on business. On fast Sunday I found my way to the Manhattan Ward. I was a stranger, but I remember so clearly the testimony the young bishop bore before turning the meeting to the membership for testimony bearing. He explained that he was a student at Columbia University, working on his doctorate. He had a full-time job making a living for his young family of several children. He said in almost a pleading voice that he prayed constantly to the Lord not to release him from being bishop at least until after he had received his degree. He indicated that the blessings of the Lord had made it possible for him to be in the very highest percentile of his class. This young bishop knew as did Nephi that if he would do his part in accepting a call to serve, even though extremely difficult, the Lord would make him equal to the challenges.

This is the church of Jesus Christ. He is the head of it. Each person who is called is called for one purpose: to assist the Savior in bringing about his work and his glory, which he said was to "bring to pass the immortality and eternal life of man." (Moses 1:39.) What greater opportunity or blessing could come to one than this? This is why we are taught to accept every call that comes to us through the priesthood.

Notwithstanding this, on the rare occasion when the one extending the call may not know of some personal situation, it is not inappropriate to explain it to him. After he is fully acquainted with all factors, if he still desires that we serve, I believe it is our duty to respond affirmatively.——*Bishop Victor L. Brown*

What can be done to make gospel lessons more interesting?

One of my favorite aphorisms goes something like this: "The ideal teaching situation consists of Mark Hopkins sitting on one end of a log and on the other end a student."

This remark originated in a speech delivered by James A. Garfield in 1871. Garfield was a student of Mark Hopkins, the latter having served with distinction as professor of philosophy at Williams College for over fifty years. To President Garfield, Mark Hopkins was the symbol of great teaching. Interestingly, as I have investigated the life of Mark Hopkins, I have found that the paramount quality of his teaching was love.

From this and many other examples and personal experiences, I am convinced that the best way to secure an interesting lesson is for a student to sit on the "other end of a log" with a great teacher who exemplifies love. The first requisite, then, is to have the right kind of a teacher in the classroom.

None of us who are gospel teachers are as effective as we might be or ought to be. For this reason the Lord has blessed us with the teacher development and meetinghouse library programs. Through the participation of the teacher in the basic course, inservice lessons, supervision in teaching, and appropriate use of instructional materials from the meetinghouse library, lessons can't help but become more interesting. So may I suggest that all teachers and potential teachers, including youth, take advantage of teacher development classes and meetinghouse library services.

A common saying that I have heard expressed throughout the Church is: "It is not my purpose to entertain students but to teach the gospel." When one stops to think about it, this statement is inaccurate and probably even contributes to poor teaching. Let me show you why.

My *American College Dictionary* defines entertainment as follows: "To receive or admit with a view to consider and decide; to take into consideration. To keep, hold, or maintain in the mind with favor; to harbor; cherish. To *engage the attention of,* with anything that causes the time to pass pleasantly." (Italics added.) And within a teaching situation we might add: to entertain is to make a lesson interesting, for the dictionary defines *interesting* as "engaging attention." With these definitions, shouldn't teachers make an effort to entertain students?

I have observed that frequently when a teacher announces he does not intend to entertain anybody, he is looking for an excuse for his lack of preparation.

Teachers should be cautioned not to entertain simply for entertainment's sake or for amusement only. The stimulating ideas and techniques a teacher uses should be directed toward carrying out an objective that will change the lives of students. Gospel lessons should accomplish more than simply be interesting. They should change people's lives and cause them to keep the Lord's commandments. But I believe that the way a teacher changes people's lives for good is by entertaining them through spiritual, social, or intellectual experiences, and all of this, ideally, within a loving relationship.

We have been discussing what might be done with a teacher to make gospel lessons more interesting. But another requisite of an interesting lesson that comes off with impact is to have good students as well as a good teacher. Even the most qualified and best-prepared teacher can go down in failure if he has a classroom of incorrigible rescals who are bent on being the devil's advocates. Every student in a gospel classroom has the responsibility of helping his teacher succeed. An unfortunate condition in all too many classrooms exists with some students who attempt to be self-appointed entertainers during lessons, disrupting and robbing everyone who is present of meaningful learning experiences. Interesting lessons call for attentive, contributing class members.

The ideal teaching situation to make gospel lessons interesting and meaningful is an outstanding Latter-day Saint teacher on one end of the log—a teacher who knows how to entertain and love—and on the other end, students who are supportive and eager to learn, with reciprocating love for the teacher.—— *Charles R. Hobbs*

How can I profit more from stake conference? Lately I've begun to feel that going to conference is a waste of my time.

Conferences in the Church are special occasions when members and nonmembers alike gather and glean strength from one another and from the speakers. The words of truth delivered there can benefit you in your church callings as well as in personal matters.

Unfortunately, some people who attend both local and general conferences feel that there is really nothing there for them. Usually the blame is placed on the speakers, but why, if the speakers are at fault, does one person go home dissatisfied while another, who was seated close-by, find that it was one of the best conferences he has ever attended? The problem is not in the speaker but in the listener.

Certainly speakers do have a great obligation to prepare to speak. They should follow the Lord's admonition to "teach one another the doctrine of the kingdom." Those who do so diligently are promised that grace will attend them. (D&C 88:77-78.) In their preparations the speakers should assess the needs of the congregation and make themselves receptive to the promptings of the Spirit. But how often is an excellent sermon not delivered because of the unreceptive attitude of the audience? When the audience has been expecting and praying for inspiration, speakers often find that they speak with power beyond their natural capacities. It seems that the spiritual growth, inspiration, and satisfaction derived from conference are largely a personal matter.

Some have expressed regret that General Authorities are no longer able to attend local conferences with the same regularity that they used to. We know that the growth of the Church makes this impossible. Remember that Jesus said, "Verily, verily, I say unto you, He that receiveth whomseover I send receiveth me; and he that receiveth me receiveth him that sent me." (John 13:20.) In other words, if a person does not value and respect local speakers in their assignments, the Lord's Spirit will not be with that person.

Exactly how can the listener profit more from conference?

First, he needs to prepare his mind for the conference by being expectant, receptive, optimistic. He should have been obeying the commandments and have been endeavoring to put into practice those items of counsel imparted at the last conference. As important as it is to attend conferences, more important are the periods of faithfulness during the intervening months. "And it shall come to pass, that inasmuch as they are faithful, and exercise faith in me, I will pour out my Spirit upon them in the day that they assemble themselves together." (D&C 44:2.)

In addition, going to the Lord in prayer with regard to special problems or needs, as well as fasting, can be beneficial to you, to the speaker, and to the others in the congregation.

Those who thus assemble to receive the Lord's will concerning them are told that "this is pleasing unto your Lord, and the angels rejoice over you; the alms of your prayers have come up into the ears of the Lord of Sabaoth, and are recorded in the book of the names of the sanctified, even them of the celestial world." (D&C 88:1-2.)

If you give some thought to your preparation, the Lord's will can be revealed to you, and conferences can become meaningful events in your life.——*Richard H. Morley*

Index

Aaronic Priesthood, 44-47
Academic learning, 34-35
Affection, 58-59
Anderson, Arthur S., answer by,
    41-43
Arnold, Marilyn, answers by, 59-60,
    60-62
Art, modern, 26-27
Artists, experiences necessary to,
    23-25
Awareness, 30-31

Backman, Robert L., answers by, 44-
    47, 75-77
Bahr, Howard M., answer by, 16-21
Ballif, Jae R., quotation from, 31
Bar of iron, 100
Bassett, Arthur R., answer by, 22-23
Bell, Alexander Graham, 101
Bennett, William H., answer by,
    100-1
Berrett, William E., quotation from,
    90
Bishop: Aaronic Priesthood and, 45;
    to help drug users, 50; in
    Manhattan Ward, 105-6
Bishops court, 28, 29
Blanch, Mae, answer by, 14-15
Blind faith, 4
Bonnell, John S., quotation from,
    101
Born in the covenant, 81-82
Borrowing, 35-36
Bridal gown, 79-80
Brown, Hugh B., quotation from,
    33
Brown, Victor L., answers by, 12-13,
    91-92, 105-6
Brown, Victor L., Jr., answers by,
    49-51, 51-52
Business interests of Church, 97-98

Caffeine, 96
Callings in Church, 105-6
Cameron, J. Elliott, answer by, 34-35
Campaigns for causes, 12-13
Cancellation of sealing, 81-82
Cannon, Kenneth L., study by, 84-85
Celestial relationship, 63
Cheerleaders, 59-60
Child, Hortense H., answer by, 87-89
Children born in the covenant, 81-82
Christensen, Alberta H., answer by,
    86-87
Christensen, Joe J., answers by,
    35-36, 58-59
Christiansen, ElRay L., answer by,
    8-11
Church court, 28-29
Church of Jesus Christ of Latter-day
    Saints: campaigns under direction
    of, 12-13; business interests of,
    97-98; callings in, 105-6;
    conferences in, 108-9
Clarke, Mary, answer by, 77-78
Cola drinks, 96
College, 11-12, 33
Companies owned by Church, 97
Conferences, 108-9
Conscience, and Light of Christ, 6-8
Conservatism, political, 15-16
Courts, Church, 28-29
Courtship, 44, 63-64
Covey, Stephen R., answer by, 92-95
Crane, Stephen, quotation from, 17
Creativity, 23-25, 25-26
Cullimore, James A., answer by,
    81-82

Dating: appropriate age for, 52-54;
    nonmembers, 55; prayers in, 55-
    57; standards in, 58-59
Deacons quorum president, 44

Debt, 35-36
Dental student, 74
Divorce, 81-82, 84-85
Dress standards, 59-60
Drugs, 49-51, 51-52
Dunn, Loren C., answers by, 40-41, 99
Durham, G. Homer, answers by, 1-3, 15-16
Durrant, Will and Ariel, quotation from, 59

Ear piercing, 102-3
Eberhard, Ernest L., Jr., answers by, 43-44, 47-49
Ecology, 17, 20-21
Edmunds, Jasmine R., 79-80
Ellsworth, Homer, answer by, 103-5
Edmunds, John K., answer by, 70-74
Education: value of, 30-32; necessity of, 33; academic and religious, 34-35
Einstein, 101
Endowment, 67-68, 70-74
Engagement, 63, 64
Entertainment, 107
Ethnocentrism, 16-17
Excommunication, 28-30
Existentialism, 14-15
Experience to artists, 23-25
Extremism, 25-26, 94

Faith, 4, 105-6
Fanaticism, 25-26, 94
Fast offerings, 97
Fasting, 93-95
Featherstone, Vaughn J., answer by, 52-54
First Presidency letter concerning tithing, 91
Food storage, 98-99
Free agency, 103-5

Garfield, James A., quotation from, 106

God, 9, 11-12. *See also* Savior
Going steady, 53

Hanks, Marion D., answer by, 36-37
Harris, Russell C., answer by, 89-91
Hemingway, Ernest, quotation from, 100
High council court, 28, 29
Hinckley, Gordon B., answer by, 39-40
Hitchhiking, 60-62
Hobbs, Charles R., answer by, 106-8
Hopkins, Mark, 106
Hypnotism, 103-5

Immaturity, 83
Income, 91
Intellectual pursuits, 30-32
Interest, 91
Investment, 35-36

Jardine, Winnifred, answer by, 98-99
Jarman, Dean, answer by, 6-8
Jeppsen, Malcolm S., answer by, 67-70
Jesus Christ, 8-9. *See also* Savior

Kapp, Ardeth G., answer by, 55-57
Kerr, William Rolfe, answer by, 62-64
Keys given to missionaries, 37-38
Kimball, Spencer W., answer by, 38-39; quotation from, 53
Knowledge, 34-35

Lee, Harold B., quotations from, 5, 69-70, 72, 87
Liberalism, political, 15-16
Life, meaning of, 14-15
Light of Christ, 6-8
Listeners, 108-9
Love in teaching, 106-7

Lucifer, 8-10, 25-26
Lyman, Francis M., quotation from, 103-4
Lynn, Karen, answer by, 30-32

Man, 14-15, 19
Manhattan Ward, 105-6
Marriage: after a mission, 43-44; mate selection for, 64-66; temple, 67-70; ceremony in temple, 75-77; dress for temple, 79-80; early, 82-86; and the single woman, 86-87
Maryon, Edward D., answer by, 26-27
Mate selection, 64-66
McKay, David O., quotation from, 53
Merrill, Roger, answer by, 3-5
Mind-control, 103-5
Mission, 39-40, 43-44
Missionaries: receive keys, 37-38; assignment of, 38-39; waiting for, 40-41; girls as, 41-43; given endowment, 72
Missionary Executive Committee, 39
Modern art, 26-27
Modesty, 59-60
Money, borrowing, 35-36
Moral cleanliness, 68
Morley, Richard H., answer by, 108-9

Occupation, 36-37
Opinions, 47-49
Overpopulation, 17-21

Parents, 47-49
Pearson, Carol Lynn, answer by, 23-25
Petersen, Mark E., quotation from, 53
Peterson, H. Burke, answer by, 95-96
Piercing ears, 102-3

Playing cards, 100-1
Points of view, 47-49
Politics, 15-16
Prayer, 3-5, 55-57
Priesthood, 37-38, 44-47, 87-89

Radio receiver, 5
Rawson, J. Murray, answer by, 37-38
Rebaptism, 28-29
Religion, 11-12, 22, 34-35
Repentance, 27-28, 92-93
Revelation concerning temple endowment, 71
Ripley, Robert, quotation from, 100
Romney, Lenore, answer by, 55
Romney, Marion G., quotation from, 68

Sabbath day, 89-91
Sacrament, 99
Satan, 8-11, 25-26
Savior, 6-8, 49, 51. *See also* God
School, boy sees film in; 3
Sealing, temple, 75-77, 81-82
Sharp, Marianne C., answer by, 102-3
Siddoway, William R., answer by, 33
Simpson, Robert L., answer by, 27-30
Smith, Joseph, quotations from, 9, 71-72
Smith, Joseph F., quotation from, 43
Smith, Joseph Fielding, quotations from, 34, 67, 87
Social Services Department, 49-50
Speakers, 108-9
Stake conferences, 108-9
Standards: contemporary, 22-23; to the artist, 24; in dating; 55, 58-59; in costuming, 59-60
Students, 98-99, 107-8
Sunday, 89-91

Talmage, James E., quotation from, 73

Tanner, N. Eldon, answer by, 97-98

Taylor, John, quotation from, 4

Taylor, John W., quotation from, 103

Teaching, 106-8

Temple: requirements for entering, 67-70; endowments in, 70-74; marriage ceremony in, 75-77; attending, for first time, 77-78; nonmembers at, 78; dress in, 79-80

Temple divorce, 81-82

Temple recommend, 67-70

Tensmeyer, Lowell G., answer by, 11-12

Testimony, 1-3, 67

Thomas, Darwin L., answers by, 64-66, 82-86

Thought, 22-23

Tithing, 91-92, 97-98

Toad, 17

Truth, 14-15, 31

Turner, Rodney, answer by, 25-26

Vocation, 36-37

Wedding, dress, 79-80

Welfare services program, 50, 97

Wesley, Susannah, quotation from, 90

Word of Wisdom, 95-96

Young, Brigham, quotations from, 2, 68

Youth campaigns, 12-13